ASPECTS OF WAKEFIELD

ASPECTS *of* WAKEFIELD

Discovering Local History

Edited by
Kate Taylor

Series Editor
Brian Elliott

Wharncliffe Publishing

First Published in 1998 by
Wharncliffe Publishing
an imprint of
Pen and Sword Books Limited,
47 Church Street, Barnsley,
South Yorkshire. S70 2AS

Copyright © Wharncliffe Publishing 1998

For up-to-date information on other titles produced under the
Wharncliffe imprint, please telephone or write to:

> **Wharncliffe Publishing**
> **FREEPOST**
> **47 Church Street**
> **Barnsley**
> **South Yorkshire S70 2BR**
> **Telephone (24 hours): 01226 - 734555**

ISBN: 1-871647-41-X

A CIP catalogue record of this book is available from the
British Library

Cover illustration: *Marygate,* 1901 by Louisa Fennell.

Printed in Great Britain by
St. Edmundsbury Press, Bury St. Edmunds, Suffolk.

CONTENTS

INTRODUCTION

by Kate Taylor

The *Aspects* series of books on local history is now well established but this is the first volume to focus on Wakefield and the surrounding area. The series was founded in 1993 with the publication of *Aspects of Barnsley* edited by Brian Elliott. This proved so successful that further volumes followed rapidly and a fifth volume of Barnsley essays is to appear in 1998. Meanwhile the first *Aspects of Rotherham*, edited by Mel Jones, appeared in 1995, followed by *Aspects of Doncaster* in 1997 and *Aspects of Leeds* early in 1998. Brian Elliott is now the General Editor of the series. The books, which cover a very wide range of topics, embrace work not only by well-established local historians but also by people who have never previously written for publication.

Rhubarb has been since the late nineteenth century a significant feature of the Wakefield-Morley-Leeds landscape and of the local economy. Today rhubarb-growing is a key element in Wakefield's tourism strategy. Yet no detailed history of the culture of rhubarb locally has hitherto been written and John Goodchild's essay, based largely on primary source material in the John Goodchild Collection, fills this gap. John has also contributed an account of a unique, and increasingly resented, aspect of the *Wakefield Inclosure Act* of 1793 whereby those who were allotted land under the Inclosure were rendered liable to pay for damages incurred by those who mined the lord of the manor's coal. This penalty was quashed only when Ronald Swinden, himself instructed to make payment in the 1970s, took up the landholders' cause. Here history was being made and he gives his own account both of this achievement and of his rôle in assisting householders to combat demands for another payment – for making up their streets.

Mining has until recently been another feature of the local landscape. Keith Wainwright's account of one of the area's many highly original and ingenious figures, Bramwell Pashley, focuses on one-man enterprises in small-scale coalmining.

Wakefield has provided many subjects for topographers and other artists, some of whom have captured the industrial or commercial scene, but many of whom have been drawn to its older properties, especially the surviving, albeit largely rebuilt in the 1840s, Chantry Chapel on Wakefield Bridge. Antonino Vella's essay provides the first comprehensive account of these 'images of Wakefield', many of which are in the collection at Wakefield Art Gallery.

Two essays focus on very different aspects (although perhaps in some way related) of Ossett which could perhaps be characterised as the saintly and the sinful! Ann Barnes has made a study of an unusual topic for local historians - bastardy - questioning whether in the early nineteenth century there were clusters of families in Ossett given to producing children out of wedlock. David Scriven writes about the later nineteenth century temperance movement as it affected the Ossett community.

Temperance was certainly an influence upon the members of Wakefield's New Scarborough Adult School who pioneered the area's first Garden City on a site just off Dewsbury Road. Privet hedges, and no public houses, were fundamental to the scheme as Kate Taylor notes. In a companion piece to her essay, Pearl Putscher recalls a period of her own childhood in this Garden City as a member of a teenagers' club in the years of the Second War. The enterprise and innocence of this small group are remarkable and might seem today to be part of a very different world albeit a mere fifty years ago. Pearl refers to an outing to Woolley Dam. Brian Elliott has traced this former mill dam and later leisure facility both on the ground and through primary source material.

A different, and only short-lived, development taking place at the same time as the Garden City, was that at Lofthouse Park where, as a boost to traffic, the local tramways company founded an entertainment centre in 1908. Peter Wood's essay recounts the palmy days of the Park and its subsequent history as an internment camp in the Great War. Peter's other essay here is also about leisure – the activities at a field in Belle Vue, home from the 1870s to Wakefield Trinity Rugby football but also the venue for anything from a Wild West Show to a moslem Mela.

Two entirely different but both very important developments in Wakefield in the twentieth century are related here – the origin and growth of the Wakefield Shirt Company, one of Wakefield's major employers, and the realisation of five nurses' dream to provide a hospice in Wakefield. The latter is the subject of a detailed and factual account by Dr Alan Kirkbright, himself closely involved in the hospice movement.

If there is to be an *Aspects of Wakefield 2* more contributors will be needed. Anyone interested in submitting existing research or undertaking a new project is invited in the first instance to contact Kate Taylor, c/o Wharncliffe Publishing Ltd, 47 Church Street, Barnsley, S70 2AS

1. THE STORY OF RHUBARB

by John Goodchild, M. Univ

THE STORY OF RHUBARB GROWING in the West Riding is a curious one, and also one peculiarly difficult to elucidate because nothing is recorded of its history in connected form, and its growers were also small-scale market gardeners who kept little in the way of records. So it is from passing references that its story must be gathered, and from indirect sources of a considerable variety. To discover something of its history, the present writer has had to search newspapers, farm leases, sale particulars, maps, tax returns, ratebooks, trade directories, the few technical papers written on its cultivation, old encyclopaedias and more, and he has used personal reminiscences to a small degree too. On the other hand, the total impact on the Wakefield-Leeds-Morley triangle in which rhubarb has largely been grown locally has been economically considerable, and its physical impact can still be appreciated, with its unique forcing sheds and the rhubarb plants out in the fields in an area stretching in concentrated form from Thornes in the south to north of the River Aire and west to Morley (Figure 1).

The uses of the plant have been varied and have included medicinal purposes, use as an ornamental garden plant, as a fruit (although rhubarb is in fact a vegetable), for canning, for bulking-out jams, and, forced, its sale in grocers' shops and supermarkets in our own day in its red and golden-headed form.

It is believed to have been in 1732 that specimens of the rhubarb plant were first sent from Russia, where it was being cultivated, to Paris and to London, and to the great botanist Linnaeus in Uppsala. These specimens were for scientific botanical purposes and by 1765 the plant was being grown in the Botanical Gardens in Edinburgh and a paper was then read to a scientific audience. But the native rhubarb plant grows in Mongolia, between Russia and China, and

Figure 1. Rhubarb sheds at Grandstand Farm, Wrenthorpe, now part of the Wakefield 41 Industrial Estate. *D Macauley.*

also in China near to its Tibetan border, and from ancient times the roots, dried out and threaded on strings, were sent to the west for medicinal purposes – for use as a laxative. By the eighteenth century they came from Mongolia via St Petersburg, or from China via Canton, in vessels of the East India Company. What was brought was a dried substance, bright buff yellow in colour, which was then ground and used for medicinal purposes mixed with various liquids for internal use.

The earliest of the great modern encyclopaedias is that edited by Rev Dr Abraham Rees, a Unitarian minister, and published in forty-five volumes between 1805 and 1819. Its contribution on rhubarb covers several pages. As a medicine rhubarb was being dispensed in this country in the sixteenth century and of course it continued to be used as a medicine in modern times. It was in this capacity that it seems first to appear in Yorkshire. This writer has been unable to find any reference to it in the regional newspapers, the *Leeds Mercury* and the *Leeds Intelligencer*, in the 1760s, 1770s and 1780s, but there are references in the 1790s. In June 1793 the *Leeds Intelligencer* tells us that the Society of Arts at their annual meeting in London presented a silver medal to Thomas Halley of Pontefract 'for an account how to cure rhubarb' and in July 1797 the paper refers to the Society of Arts awarding a gold medal to the Reverend James Stillingfleet of Hotham near Market Weighton 'for the culture and cure of the true rhubarb', i.e. for its medicinal use.

By the beginning of the nineteenth century at the latest, rhubarb plants were being cultivated in the West Riding, probably primarily for ornamental garden use, but possibly also for eating and perhaps for supply as medicinal raw materials. The plants were supplied by men who ran gardens for the supply of plants, trees, fruit and flowers to the more well-to-do, but by the 1840s at the latest, rhubarb was being grown by market gardeners, of whom there were vast numbers in the Wakefield area from the beginning of the century. These market gardeners were supplying rhubarb primarily, if not entirely, as a fruit – for stewing and for making into pies.

In the West Riding rhubarb was available from the early nineteenth century from the chemist for medicinal purposes, as a purgative. In Wakefield, for example, in 1813, John Potter, a chemist and druggist, supplied Samuel Holdsworth of Crigglestone Cliffe, dyer and gentleman, with two and a half ounces of 'True Turkey Rhubarb' at a cost of 6s 3d, while rhubarb plants were cultivated as garden plants in gentlemen's gardens (Figure 2). In 1822 John Lee, the solicitor and landowner of St John's, was supplied by Barratt's Gardens, also at St.John's, with '2 Large Rhubarb' at a cost of a shilling.

About 1820 or 1830 it became obvious that it was possible to provide artificial conditions for growing rhubarb plants out of season, and the experiments were of a very *ad hoc* nature – some were grown in a spare room of a market gardener's house. Then by about 1850 roots were being taken into darkened and heated greenhouses in winter and from the crowns an artificial growth forced, which sold well locally, although the output was tiny. But the first evidence of cultivation on a commercial scale of rhubarb stools is on the smallholding of Benjamin Briggs at Thornes in the mid 1840s. Briggs came from a family of market gardeners – at that time described as gardeners – and there was one of the same name, a market gardener and owner of land at Westgate, who voted at the great Yorkshire election of 1807 and is hence listed in the poll book. There was a Richard Briggs, a market gardener at Thornes, who occupied land there in 1804 and whose widow died in 1830 aged 78. There were others too, at Potovens and Newton, all market gardeners of the surname of Briggs.　But our Benjamin Briggs was a market gardener at Thornes by 1824 when he advertised (as was then legally necessary) that he had set spring guns in his gardens at Thornes, while in 1822 he had been fined for shooting a hare. He was also landlord of the *Spangled Bull Inn* at Thornes, now the *Queen's Arms,* and when he made his will in December 1844 he described himself therein as innkeeper and farmer. He died in January 1845 with total assets of £430 19s 9d (including £10 in wines and spirits, £131 0s 7d in horses and farming stock and £190 3s 2d in stock in trade). His funeral costs totalled £20. His landlords were Henry Lumb the Wakefield solicitor and Benjamin Gaskell of Thornes House. It is possible to work out from his executorship papers, which survive, some considerable detail of Briggs' actual production: he occupied under Mr Gaskell some 60 and a half acres at Willow Hall Farm and White House

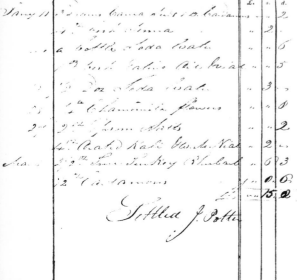

Figure 2. John Potter's bill of 1813 which includes an item for supplying Samuel Holdsworth with two and a half ounces of 'True Turkey Rhubarb'.
The John Goodchild Collection.

and grew large acreages of potatoes, wheat, savoys,   carrots, onions, grass and broccoli, with smaller areas of cabbage and herbs. A list of his equipment includes no forcing containers – only garden pots – but a list of the crops on Henry Lumb's land shows his use of manure, lime and guano, and heating, and his use of glass frames and production of lettuce, parsley, savoys, cabbage plants, curled greens, flowering broccoli, standard and gooseberry trees, but most interestingly his possession of what are described as:

29 Victoria Rhuebarb Stools planted in 1846

18 Stools of Rheubarb (Figure 3).

The medicinal use of rhubarb continued, and evidence at a coroner's inquest in 1853 refers to a Wakefield woman getting 'a rhubarb powder' for a bad stomach at Hodgson's shop in the town. Curiously there is no Hodgson, chemist,   in the 1853 directory but there is a John Hodgson, herbalist, at 42 Northgate.

It was possibly in the 1870s that the long, low, black-roofed forcing sheds which are now so characteristic of the industry were first used in the West Riding, and the success of the forcing of rhubarb on a modest scale, on smallholding farms, and at a modest cost, became apparent, and many market gardeners went in for forced rhubarb cultivation. But it is not until the 1880s that forcing rhubarb in dark and heated sheds is referred to in manuscripts. There is the account book of Mrs Mary Ramsden, widow of Benjamin Ramsden of Brandy Carr Farm, leased from February 1870 at a substantial £210 a year; his predecessor William Ramsden had occupied over 31 acres here in 1843, and a John Ramsden who made his will in January 1840 as a gardener of Brandy Carr may have been the same John Ramsden described as a collier of Brandy Carr in 1811. Mrs Ramsden had become a widow in 1886. She records:

1886 Comenced to get Rhub Roots up on the 20th of Nov Fired on the 2nd of Dec begun to pull on the 11th Jany 1887.

Reference is also made to buying rhubarb mats in January 1887 at 7s, in April 1887 'paid to Mr Myers for Soot' £3, and paid for manure in mid 1886 and March 1887, and Amos Pickersgill was paid for hoeing. Men's and women's wages are recorded from 1 May 1886 to 30 April 1847: in winter wages were much lower than in the summer. In winter the total wages paid could sink as low as £4 10s 5d, but from the beginning of June to the end of August 1887, they rose to double figures – the largest £17 10s in a week.

'Loads' were sent off on Tuesdays, Thursdays and Saturdays, with values of from £2.5s to £25 10s – this last on winter Saturdays only.

Payments were made to the Great Northern Railway at Lofthouse and some to the Midland Railway (Birmingham and possibly Sheffield?). Domestic references mention the boys' and Rosalie's railway passes, and dress dyeing. Mrs Ramsden took a new lease of her farm from March 1887 but a trade directory of the Bradford, Halifax and Wakefield area of February 1887 also refers to a Joseph Savile Ramsden of Vine Cottage, Brandy Carr, nurseryman, florist and fruit grower, and market gardeners include Jesse Ramsden of Brandy Carr and Beeston.

Mr Sam Richardson, of Springfield Farm near Wrenthorpe, who was born about 1900, and once had his own rhubarb-growing business, said that one of the Ramsden family with whom he was friendly thought that it was about 1860 that one of the Ramsdens had accidentally discovered the forcing of rhubarb using a container put over a root.

Figure 3. A valuation of 1847crops and trees in plots of ground at Thornes formerly tenanted by Benjamin Briggs and referring to '29 Victorian Rhuebarb stools' and '18 Stools of Rhuebarb'. *The John Goodchild Collection.*

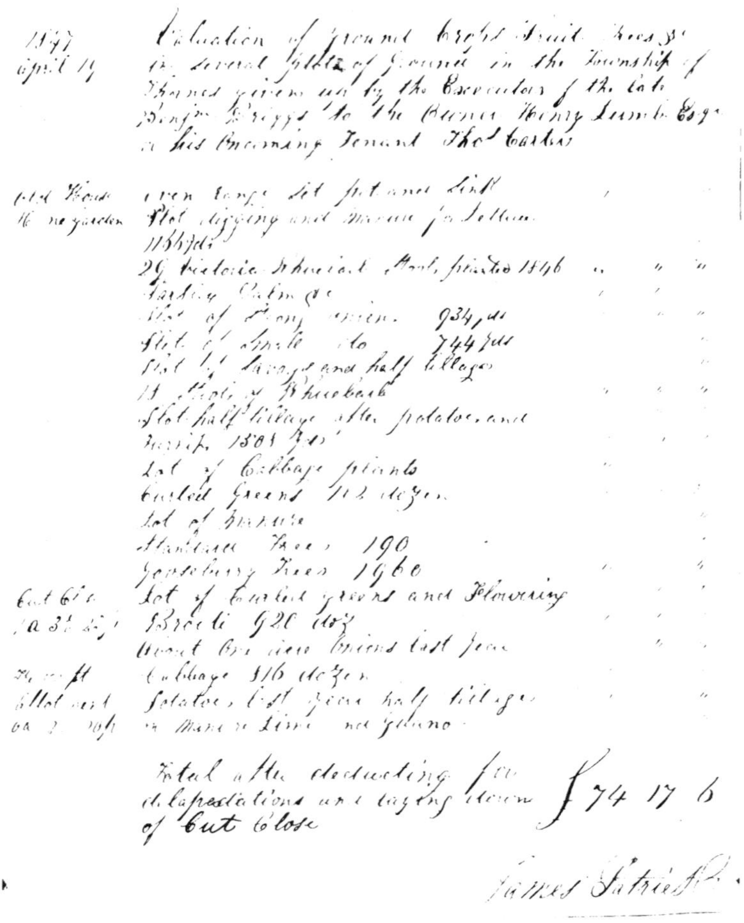

Of the 76 market gardeners listed in the area of the 1887 textile area trade directory, 44, or some 58 percent, were in the Wakefield area, and a majority of those were in Stanley:

Brandy Carr   2
Outwood 7
Stanley   9
Kirkhamgate 2
Carr Gate 2
Wrenthorpe   5
Bottomboat   2
Ouchthorpe Lane 1
Newmarket Gate   1
Broom Hall 1
Lake Lock 1 = 33 in all

Horbury   5
Sandal 2
Wakefield 1
Flanshaw Lane 1
Thornes 2 = 11

Rhubarb forcing was certainly developing by the 1880s and in July 1889, when the Earl of Cardigan's estates in Wakefield and New Park were offered for sale by auction, lot 32, Low Laithes Farm, included a brick and slated

> *maltkiln, now converted into a chaff-cutting house: with Rhubarb Forcing House over, and another Rhubarb Forcing House adjoining*

and C S Robson had been the tenant. The farm covered some 90 acres and had rented at £95 a year, although there was some re-lotting for this sale.

The Ordnance Survey re-visited this part of the West Riding from the late 1880s and obviously recorded in map form all buildings then on the ground. In the Stanley and Outwood area, large buildings which may be purpose-built rhubarb sheds are shown at Bottomboat, opposite to Iveridge Hall off Aberford Road, beyond the present M62, at Lake Lock and, the largest and most ambitious of all, at the top of Jerry Clay Lane at Brandy Carr (the Ramsden sheds). Those near Iveridge Hall, at Bottomboat and at Jerry Clay Lane are now green field sites with no evidence of any buildings but at Lake Lock half of a very long, aisled, timber-built, rhubarb shed survives (Figure 4). This may be the oldest surviving rhubarb shed in the West Riding. It has been recently recorded in photographs but it is in a very dilapidated state and needs thorough recording and measuring. Incidentally, when the Ordnance Survey resurveyed the area after 1900 many more sheds for forcing rhubarb existed and were duly shown on the new maps and of course something of the physical spread of the industry can be gauged from the various editions of the OS.

Unfortunately for the historian, rhubarb sheds were regarded as agricultural buildings so that they are not listed in rate books, where they were taken with all buildings in with the value of the land as Gache's *Guide to the Law of Local and Parochial Rates* tells us, nor were they subject to the passing of plans by local authorities. The writer has searched all the minute books of the Wakefield Rural Sanitary Authority which covered the rural area widely around Wakefield and which had to pass and approve all other plans for new buildings, but there are no references to rhubarb sheds. Equally, the trade directories of 1861, 67, 77, 87, 97 and 1902 have all been searched without any reference to rhubarb growing: this is because the cultivation of rhubarb was only one of the concerns of market gardeners, who are listed as such. An 1892 directory does refer to one Batley rhubarb grower, and one of 1911 covering Leeds mentions another at Stourton Lodge near Thwaite Gate.

Now why did the rhubarb growing industry flourish more here in the area between Wakefield, Leeds and Morley, than elsewhere in the country and why, indeed, was more rhubarb grown here than in the whole of the United States? There were a number of interacting reasons, essentially connected to landholding, to the local soil types, to rainfall and to markets for rhubarb. In most of the area farms were small, and market gardening offered better financial results on a smallholding than did growing cereal crops, while there were, of course, large populations close by to be served with eating rhubarb through their flourishing markets as well as vegetable corner shops, and the tradition of market gardening for local markets was a very old one. Then there was the suitability of the soil: the rhubarb plant loves moisture and needs a plentiful supply of water during its growth, while the local clay subsoils hold the moisture in the surface soil well; a free drainage is necessary as water must not lie in the top soil layers, and the local countryside is, of course, undulating. In the area were large and cheap supplies of ashes to help with free drainage and these were spread nine to twelve inches thick on land intended for rhubarb cultivation and ploughed in, ashes being brought in and spread four to eight inches deep every further three or four years.

Figure 4. The remains of an early (perhaps the earliest local) rhubarb shed, at Lake Lock, near Wakefield, 1996. *The John Goodchild Collection.*

Then there were ample supplies of horse manure to aid the rhubarb crop, ample shoddy refuse and ample sewage sludge, all for humus and manure, while to heat the forcing sheds, there was low cost and low grade fuel amply available from the local pits. The rhubarb crop prefers acidic conditions so waste deposit (soot) from the local consumption by furnaces was just suitable, and we have seen Mrs Widow Ramsden paying for soot for her crop. In fact it was claimed that in the industrial period some ten cwts of soot were deposited naturally on each acre in this area during each year. Again, a smoke-laden atmosphere screens the sun, and in consequence less moisture is absorbed into the air, and the dirty atmosphere was believed to force the rhubarb root tops to die back early enough to be lifted and housed in the autumn. Another reason claimed at the time was that in the 1880s when rhubarb forcing came into existence on a commercial scale, there had been some ten years of bad summers which had forced the local market gardeners who had grown strawberries and other fruit to turn to another crop more suited to the weather conditions of the period; again rhubarb needs frosts to create the conditions in the root which can lead to the forcing of tender growth in dark, wet and warmed sheds.

So far as markets for the produce were concerned, there were the ample local markets and shops mentioned, and a new market in London developed. It is claimed that it was in 1879 that the first rhubarb special train ran to London, and such trains continued until about 1964, after which road transport was entirely used. Every night between January and March, laden hampers of rhubarb for Covent Garden Market were taken to the local station on the GN Leeds-Wakefield-Kings Cross route, to a train called the Rhubarb Special, and sometimes two trains were needed, carrying 80 or 100 tons. Waggons were loaded at Morley Top Station, at East Ardsley, Lofthouse, Stanley and Wakefield, and the train collected the trucks into one load for London. It is remembered that the train left East Ardsley at 9.12pm during the season. Up to 1940, most of the rhubarb was carried in hampers of four to six dozen bundles, regarded as a handy-sized pack for a shop.

An annual rhubarb show was organized by the Leeds and District Market Gardeners and Rhubarb Growers Association, usually held in Leeds, and staged from about 1920, where rhubarb was the only exhibit.

During the Second World War, a national shortage of fruit led to a demand for rhubarb above the usual, and to an increased price and profit for the growers, even though the government restricted the acreage of rhubarb grown to provide for more basic crops' cultivation, and there was a Maximum Prices Order to prevent the worst of profit-making, not revoked until the end of 1946, when, because of the continuing shortage of fresh fruit, the demand for rhubarb continued strong and prices and profits were still high. But as more of other fruit began to be grown, the demand for rhubarb nationally declined from 1947, and prices and profits dropped markedly. In some local townships as much as 40 percent of the arable area was devoted to rhubarb between the wars, especially in West Ardsley, Morley and Outwood. During the First War rhubarb had again been given an impetus by the national war situation: a jam factory, using rhubarb as a filler to the jam fruits, existed at Canal Lane, Stanley (built originally as a rope and twine mill), but this closed down for making jam early in the 1920s; green, unforced rhubarb was used, as it was by Moorhouse's jam factory in Old Lane at Beeston, which took rhubarb from the Tingley area, and R S Dyson of Wakefield traded in jam made with rhubarb by John Smith of Shipley, a large wholesale manufacturer.

The supermarkets became after 1950 a new and very major forced rhubarb market, and the canners were another, probably of earlier origin. After 1950 the rhubarb industry was to be faced with new factors: lack of cheap and skilled labour willing to undertake the heavy and specialist work of handling rhubarb crowns and filling them into forcing sheds; the increased cost of fuel, whether coal or the newer use of coke, or other heat sources; the costs of new shed building; lower returns on production; new markets; and last, but not least, new demands on the land hitherto used for rhubarb growing – for industrial development and housing in particular.

It must be remembered too that while the West Riding grew most forced rhubarb, and forcing was its speciality as against producing green, field rhubarb, there were other areas in this country which also grew the crop. In 1938, for example, just before the new conditions of the Second War, the West Riding grew some 47 percent of the national total, but Lancashire grew 7 percent, the Glasgow area the best part of 12 percent, Essex nearly 8 percent around Rainham and Ockinden, and Cheshire some $3^1/_2$ per cent with other smaller areas. In the West Riding rhubarb cultivation covered in

1913 3,170 acres
1938 3,818 acres
1948 4,024 acres
1954 2,849 acres

In the early 1950s, 46 percent of production was from small

smallholdings of between five and 30 acres in the West Riding. National production was increasing after the Second War, but prices were falling:

Before war	8400a under rhubarb, yielding	72,000 tons	value £1,500,000	price £7 10s per ton
1941-2	6800	67,000	1,600,000	£25
1945-6	7600	69,000	3,200,000	£46
1950-1	10300	59,000	1,300,000	£22

During the Second World War the price for rhubarb was controlled at 11d per pound wholesale and 12d retail. The situation did change from 1950, and an example of what occurred is the case of H Cartlidge (Morley) Ltd, who had probably been the largest rhubarb forcers in Yorkshire in 1950, who continued to grow greentop – ie non forced – outdoor rhubarb and had in 1979 about 120 acres of it, but converted their forcing sheds to the cultivation of turkeys, chickens and mushrooms and sold their outdoor rhubarb now to the canners.

So what of the process of forcing this vegetable, rhubarb? The plant is not propagated from seeds, but from sets – parts of developed roots. The land was prepared for cultivation by ploughing, and dressed heavily with manure, sewageworks ashes, sludge, shoddy waste, soot – up to 20cwts to the acre. Rhubarb often followed a crop of broccoli, which itself needs well-manured land, took two years in growing and was cut in May or June, leaving the ground ready for the autumn planting of rhubarb. In the field, the rhubarb sets were planted 3ft apart in rows, c5,000 to the acre. The sets were dropped in the furrow from a cart and then ploughed in. The sets were produced by splitting three-year old roots usually into four parts, but larger ones into six or seven parts. The field surface had then to be kept free of weeds by hoeing until the rhubarb plants were strong enough to overcome the weeds' competition. The crop was allowed to grow for three years before being lifted to die back for forcing in a shed. If the upper growth had been taken for greentop rhubarb, a fourth year's growth was necessary. Lifting for forcing was after the third year's growth had died back from July, when the crown was dormant, and then the set was lifted from the third week in October, partly using a special rhubarb-lifting plough. It was said that a frosted crop gave a better crop of forced rhubarb.

Then came the forcing, done in the special sheds which are still an architectural curiosity of this area. These varied in size, although the most satisfactory size was thought to be about 400 square yards, say

36 yards by 12 yards; these could also be used for mushroom-growing after the forced rhubarb had been picked. The sheds were of timber entirely, or, to prevent rotting in their lower walls, built on brick foundations or with the entire walls of brick; the walls were about 3ft 4in high and the ridge about 8 or 9ft to allow carts to enter. The roof was of wood, covered with felt and tarred overall. The building had to be as low as possible to conserve heat, but it had to allow a horse and cart to enter. Hot air flues, coal or coke fired, were used, and these were external. Any old timber was suitable for building sheds. Squire Ramsden of Brandy Carr bought the materials of the old Hippodrome Theatre in Wakefield, itself built of wood, for example, and used the rhubarb shed it provided until 1967 (Figure 5).

It took about one acre of three-year old shoots to fill a shed; sometimes two-year old roots were forced, but a greater number of them were needed. The roots were packed tightly into beds about four and a half feet wide, with narrow paths between them; no extra earth was required beyond what the roots had attached to them. All light had to be excluded, and great doors were at the ends of the buildings, which were heated to between 50 and 60 degrees Fahrenheit. Pulling the pink forced stems with their golden-yellow leaves began four or five weeks from the starting of firing, and lasted

Figure 5. A plan of the front elevation of Wakefield Hippodrome which ended its days as a rhubarb shed at Brandy Carr. *Courtesy of Kate Taylor.*

between eight and twelve weeks, according to the vigour of the roots; picking was by candlelight with special candle holders, and the crop had to be well watered each week. Some six pulls could be made; about a ton of forced rhubarb was pulled from 1,000 roots brought into the sheds. Picking was by grasping the stick at its base and twisting it so that the crown root below it was not harmed. Considerable skill was involved in deciding when each stick was ready for pulling, to provide a good appearance for the market (Figure 6).

When the roots were exhausted, they were either taken up and burnt and their ash spread onto the fields, or some were ploughed in again, or others planted out for another three years, when they were again brought into the shed and forced, producing about 75 percent of the crop of the younger roots. Plant disease was to be watched at all stages, and soil from the forcing sheds had to be carried away to land not growing rhubarb to avoid any infection, and the doors of the sheds left open to thoroughly cleanse them. Some roots were ploughed in as plant food for a following cauliflower crop.

Two varieties of rhubarb plant predominated in Victorian times: the Victoria and the Prince Albert. The Victoria must be forced after three years; the Prince Albert might be forced after two. The Victoria was a very slightly later plant, not being ready to go into the forcing shed until the beginning of December. A Cheshire grower brought out a variety he named Timperley Early which could be lifted earlier and its forced produce pulled ready for the Christmas market, but it was little grown in the West Riding by 1950.

Labour costs were, of course, of increasing significance in the costs and profits equation by 1950. In the 1920s men worked a 52-hour week for 27s 6d. After the Second World War one farmer claimed that where once his men complained of sore hands and feet, now they complained of sore bottoms from sitting on them so long! The work was partly seasonal and there was some female labour employed seasonally too. In the First World War, schoolboys as classes had earned 2d an hour picking green rhubarb in the fields for making jam for soldiers – or so they were told in regard to its destination.

The area of production of forced rhubarb – the greatest production in this area – was extensive. From Thornes in the south, where there are still working sheds, to Methley in the north east, Rothwell in the north, and Gildersome and Pudsey in the west (with outliers of single growers) was the principal area, but production centred on the area just to the north of Wakefield and it is there that so many sheds can still be seen – some in active modern use, others collapsing or collapsed.

The final section of this study deals with a number of case studies which are almost all drawn from a source never hitherto used. Some years ago the present writer was given the old minute books of the Tax Commissioners for the Lower Agbrigg Division of the West Riding: that body dealt between 1936 and 1945 – but not later – with the appeals relating to a number of rhubarb growers' taxation cases, and the incidental information given is of particular interest in illustrating some of the points already raised in this study.

One of the most detailed accounts of the organisation of a business which included rhubarb growing relates to that of W H Holmes at Woodside Farm, Lingwell Gate, a farm of 100 and a half acres, in 1934; Holmes described himself as market gardener, farmer and rhubarb grower. He was a rhubarb grower after taking over his wife's father's farm in 1924: the father-in-law had had the farm tenancy from 1909, but the first rhubarb shed was put up in 1926 and by 1937 there were three sheds, two of them 20 yards by 10, and one 40 yards by 12. Holmes claimed that he had permission from the Dealtrys (once of Lofthouse Hall nearby, and who were still local landowners) specifically to grow rhubarb. Holmes did not himself attend any market with his own produce. He employed four men and

Figure 6. Janet Oldroyd-Hulme, of E Oldroyd and Sons, with rhubarb picked by candlelight. *Wakefield MD Council.*

a boy and had a livestock of 14 cattle, 29 pigs and 6 horses. The
valuations of his stock were as follows:

	April 1933		April 1934		April 1935
	£		£		£
cattle	12	112	12	119	131
horses	4	50	4	45	45
pigs	25	24	39	46	32
poultry		2		2 10s	2 10s
rhubarb roots		384		456	507

produce area	acres	acres	acres
wheat	8	18	22 .5
oats	12 .5	7	14
straw	9	7 .5	7 .5
hay	3	4	5
rhubarb	8	12	
potatoes	4	2.5	
tares	1	1	
swedes	9	9	
cabbage	0	1.5	
savoys	0	1.5	
cauliflower	0	1	

Purchases Holmes made as follows (years ending)

	April 1934	April 1935
	£	£
cattle	17	28
rhubarb roots	183 10s	192
seeds and plants	30	44
cattle foods	140	232
manure	177	162
boxes, twine etc.	37	57

While his working costs were stated as being:

	April 1934	April 1935
	£	£
wages and national insurance	555	497
rent	95	95
water rate	14	10
carriage and haulage	186	142
repairs	42	76
blacksmith	15	

sand and cement	6	
coke	43	52*
saddlery	3	
motor expenses	31	
threshing	14	
tillage	10	
electricity	8	see above
insurance	6	6
sundries	8	6**
Income Tax	4	
mortgate interest	48	33
depreciations		
farm implements 10%	9	8
sheds 7.5%	41	29
car 25%		3
	2318 12 5d	2407 15
net profit	303 5 2d	356 13

*including coal and electricity **Milk Marketing Board levy

Holmes's sales were as follows:

years ending	April 1934 £	April 1935 £
rhubarb	1134	1321
cows and pigs	124	228
milk	165	
milk and eggs	164	
crops and general produce	192	
wheat and oats		45
potatoes and swedes		76
vegetables		40
hay and straw		8
	1815	1882

In fact in 1934 W H Holmes's business produced some 70 percent of farm sales from some 12 percent of his 100 and a half acres under rhubarb.

J H Holmes was a market gardener in Rein Road, West Ardsley, perhaps the John Henry Holmes who appears in the 1936 Directory as a farmer, of Common Side. He began business in 1907. By 1945 he had 20 acres of rhubarb, explaining that 'you place' 5,000 roots to the acre. From about 1918 he had taken £5 a week for himself, and in 1945 he still took that sum, paying £2 a week to his eldest (sic) son, and £1 to the youngest for at least the previous five years. He worked his rhubarb on a three-year system, with three sheds - he had once had four. His farm totalled 52 acres from c1930, and he grew broccoli and other greens on some 30 acres of it. Holmes commented that after the First World War, there had been a slump in rhubarb markets for some nine years, and that prices in the rhubarb trade had been controlled during the Second World War, from c1942. The war was causing him trouble in getting timber for repairs, and his business ran as follows:

| | 1943 | 1944 |
	£	£
sales	2144	1735
expenditure	1212	1483
profit	932	252

R and H Webster occupied Pitty Close Farm at Drighlington, and were described as rhubarb growers. Their father had died in 1934, and he had remembered paying as little as £3 per 1,000 for rhubarb roots in 1916. He had only two acres used for rhubarb when he started, but in 1944 the family had 40 acres dedicated to it; once they had one forcing shed, but in 1944 they had nine. They carried on their father's farm which formerly had 27 acres but now had 140. The value of their rhubarb roots, per 1,000, was:

| | 1937 | March 1943 | August 1944 | Sept. 1944 |
	£	£	£	£
1 year old	8	14	30	40
2 years old	11	17	52 10s	70
3 years old		20		

S H Cartlidge of Topcliffe Farm, West Ardsley, had bought his farm of 88 acres in June 1930 for £2,900, it having previously been known as home farm and used for the pit ponies at Topcliffe Colliery. It had no farmhouse. Some 40 acres were under rhubarb, and in 1942 Cartlidge was putting up six rhubarb sheds, each 60 yards by 12.

At Tingley, J Baldwin, a market gardener, was in business from the later 1920s and still in 1946. He had some six acres, a forcing shed 20 yards by 9, and planted 5,000 roots to the acre. He used some two and a half acres for rhubarb growing, with some 12,000 roots, some being at the three-year stage, but he did not force rhubarb in January 1945, growing some broccoli which he sold in Sheffield and living on the profit of that. He sold no roots.

S Lobley was a market gardener at 72 Britannia Road, Morley. He was in a small way of business with only 1,000 roots and a single, small shed. He had six acres but sublet some five of them. Two sons helped him, and he had begun business only in 1932. The bad weather, he claimed, in 1939 was against him, and sales in 1938-9 were only £49 19s 10d. including tomatoes grown in his own greenhouse.

Allan Gray at Blackgates Farm at Tingley claimed in 1937 that he had been hard up since 1931 when he married, but that in 1934 he took the tenancy of an additional farm, and was hence in the hands of his bank. He then had four rhubarb sheds and some new roots. In 1942 he had some 100 acres, of which 15 were market garden; he grew rhubarb and potatoes and had three forcing sheds, with ten beasts. He was a director of Allan Gray Ltd, and had a director's fee of £3 10s a week.

At Lea Royd Farm in Westerton Road, West Ardsley, J R Auty and Sons had a farm of some 40 acres and another of 94 acres at Elland. They dissolved partnership in 1937, the two sons waiving their capital and one son going to manage the farm at Elland, the other working with his father. The partners had a shop in Batley, possibly for the sale of their produce, but which was closed in March 1939, but one of the sons subsequently took a shop in Blackpool. They grew rhubarb, although by 1940 they reported that their turnover was only £2,836, where it had previously been £4,240. A new co-partnership deed seems to have been drawn up in 1941.

A substantial grower was John Edward Jaques of Rooks Nest Road (Hatfeild Farm) but living in a substantial semi-detached villa near Stanley Church at 401 Aberford Road: he announced his retirement from business in 1943. He farmed 70 acres and described himself as a market gardener; he planted 6,000 rhubarb roots to the acre, and in 1941's bad weather he lost 30,000 roots, while not one in 100 roots were fit for further use after forcing. In 1943 he took £5 a week as his wage.

What is particularly interesting about Jaques is that a number of yearly valuations of his market gardening overall survive:

	at Mar. 1940		at Mar. 1941		at Mar 1942
	£		£		£
rhubarb					
two-year old roots,					
10,000 @ £15 per 1000	285	20,000 @ £14	280	6 acres @ £100	600*
one-year old roots					
52,000 @ £10 per 1000	520	42,000 @ £10	420	3 acres @ £35	105**
new planted roots					
50,000 @ £5 per 1000	250	22,000 @ £5	110	6 acres @ £25	200***
	———		———		———
	1055		810		905
cabbage, 5 acres	60		60	4 acres	100
cauliflower	0		60		0
mint	30		10		0
onions	30		70		0
wheat	0		0		110
broccoli	0		0		90
manure and tillage	0		0		220
	———		———		———
	1,175		1,010		1,425

*36,000 roots at £16 13s 4d per 1000
**18,000 roots
***48,000 roots at £4 3s 4d per 1000

In 1945 Jaques was involved in an appeal relating to his Excess Profits Tax due; he was then retired.

A H Huddlestone was a farmer and market gardener at Methley, with two farms there and another two at Whitley Bridge, paying rents of £249 and £393. Of their total 642 acres, 250 acres were in grass, 80 in market gardens etc., and they had one acre of rhubarb sheds. Old Huddlestone was 75 in 1936 with three married sons working with him who took £3 10s each weekly. They attended the produce markets at Leeds and Bradford, and sent their produce to London. They kept only a day-book for their business and their accountant stated that he could not 'make anything out of it'. They were also registered potato merchants and one of the sons had left school at twelve and a half.

T Macauley and Sons were market gardeners at Whitehall Farm on the outskirts of Wakefield, and in 1937 their three or four farms they claimed 'keep us very busy'; too busy in fact, they claimed, to keep their financial records straight. The Macauleys came from Scotland; in 1888 one of them had emigrated to the USA but returned in 1891 or 1892 and took the Grandstand Farm on Wakefield Outwood, about 41 acres. This was bought in 1918 for £1,565. About 1914, Whitehall Farm at Newton was bought and also farmland at Durkar and Stanley. Some 450 acres were owned in all and the Macauleys were to claim to be the largest growers of forced rhubarb in the country with 29 sheds producing some 400 tons a year.

At 34 Potovens Lane at Outwood, A Yarrow had four acres used for rhubarb cultivation and did all the work himself, cultivating roots which he sold at up to £30 plus per 100 roots. He had in 1944 8,000 roots, and was selling them to E Wright. He is remembered as bad-tempered and using a crutch as he had no false leg. He built a bungalow called Iona opposite the *Drum and Monkey* public house.

The case of John R Isam, a market gardener of 14 Lee Mount Road, was one presenting unique information. His acreage of rhubarb had decreased in proportion to former crops by Government Order by 1943, from 12 acres to nine. It cost nearly £50 to plant an acre of rhubarb, the roots costing £37 10s at 5,000 to the acre plus the cost of manuring (which would last two years) and labour.

At Storiehouse Farm at Stanley, R Moore had 15 acres, two of which grew rhubarb with one forcing shed in 1940. He kept no financial records at all.

At Smalley Bight Farm at Stanley, J Wheatley had many sheds for rhubarb forcing. He paid in 1939 £15 per 1,000 for roots, and bought £60 worth but lost 30,000 roots by the frost. He had 30 acres of rhubarb and a substantial wage bill of £1,000 a year, although he claimed that he got less pay than his own workpeople. The Tax Inspector commented of Wheatley that with his 34 acres of rhubarb in 1938, worth from £50 to £200 an acre, 'he must be doing well. Some growers make "hundreds" with five acres'.

According to the 1936 Directory, A Gould at Thorpe on the Hill farmed over 150 acres. There S and T Gould had in 1941 seventeen acres of rhubarb and five forcing sheds of which only one and a half were filled. They also had 11 horses, 13 cows 19 store beasts, 37 pigs and 66 head of poultry. Rhubarb production had decreased, they claimed, due to loss of roots, and their sales had slumped in consequence.;

Year to April 1939	£1901
April 1940	841
April 1941	770

John Wild was a market gardener at Outwood. He called himself a rhubarb grower and made a substantial loss in rotten roots with some five acres of land - whether by disease or weather is not stated. He split the remaining roots, but they were not enough to provide him with sufficient to force, and he had to buy roots at a cost of £206. By 1934-35 he had a considerable bank overdraft of £1,195.

J Green was a market gardener living at 17 Lingwell Gate Lane, Outwood. In 1942 he had a total income of £961 which included property rents but incorporated a profit of £155 from market gardening of which £90 came from rhubarb. In the previous year, the rhubarb profit had been £300. He had eight milk cows, two bullocks, two horses, some poultry, three acres of rhubarb and one rhubarb shed, and employed three men.

Sources

The John Goodchild Collection, Wakefield:
Lower Agbrigg Commissioners of Taxes, minute books
Samuel Holdsworth mss
John Lee mss
Benjamin Briggs mss
Thomas Lee Coroner's Inquest deposition books
Mary Ramsden ledger
Earl of Cardigan Estate mss
Wakefield RSA minute books
Wakefield area rate books
OS 25in local sheets, various editions
West Riding trade directories
Leeds Mercury, Leeds Intelligencer, Yorkshire Post, Wakefield Express.
Rees, A, Cyclopaedia, Vol 30, (1819).
Chambers' Encyclopaedia, new ed, Vol 8, (1895).
Long, W H, Survey of Agriculture of Yorkshire, (1969).
Smith, F G, The forced Rhubarb Industry in the West Riding, (1933).
Giles, R, Forced Rhubarb in the West Riding (1970).
Tasker, J, The West Riding Rhubarb Industry, (1952).
Cowley, B, Farming in Yorkshire (1972).
Macauley, D, Comments on forced rhubarb cultivation (typescript) (1989)
Norman, B, 'Forcing Rhubarb', The Grower, 14 June 1979.
Horticulture in Britain, Part 1, Vegetables, (1967).
Produce Studies Ltd. The Market for Forced Rhubarb, (1965).
The writer has the originals or photocopies of the relevant sections of all the above printed works, and a number of additional newspaper cuttings.

Figure 7. Showing the last crop of Victoria rhubarb at Grandstand Farm, 1980. *D Macauley.*

2. IMAGES OF WAKEFIELD

by Antonino Vella

THE EARLIEST VIEWS OF THE CITY in Wakefield Art Gallery's collection can be described as topographical, ie they were intended as faithful records of actual views. For travellers and the curious in the seventeenth and eighteenth centuries visual records of far away places could only be made in the form of drawings which could then be made into engraved views at a later date. In seventeenth century England, Dutch artists started the tradition of the prospect. These drawings were done at some distance from the town and were intended to depict, if not all-embracing views, at least very comprehensive views of their subject. Topographers saw themselves as reporters as well as artists, and their work was an extension of map-making. In a sense the work of the topographer fulfilled the function that has now been taken over by the camera.

William Lodge's *Wakefield from the London Road* (not dated – probably made 1670s or 1680s, when Lodge was living in Yorkshire), records Wakefield with as much accuracy as possible, and with the inclusion of as many facts as possible about the appearance of the city at that time. The son of a local merchant, Lodge was born and educated in Leeds. He subsequently went to Jesus College, Cambridge, and eventually studied law at Lincoln's Inn. He was, however, to give up his studies in favour of travel, and went to Italy where he drew numerous views which he later etched. On his return to England he specialized in the production of topographical views in and around Leeds and York.

Figure 1. Samuel Buck, *The South Prospect of the Ruins of Sandal Castle and Town of Wakefield*, 1722, engraving. *Wakefield Art Gallery.*

The Buck brothers, Samuel (1696-1779) and Nathaniel (fl. 1727-1753), were two topographers of national importance who published numerous engraved prospects of towns and cities in this country between 1720 and 1753. One of the earliest views showing the townscape of Wakefield is Samuel Buck's engraving of *the South Prospect of the Ruins of Sandal Castle and the Town of Wakefield*, 1722 (Figure 1). Although it was the intention of such topographers as Samuel Buck to record views as accurately as possible, it must be noted that the artist in this particular instance has sacrificed accuracy in favour of an harmonious composition by neatly placing Wakefield in between the castle ruins. In reality if you stood in Buck's original vantage point, the city would be much further to the right of the picture.

Prospects of Wakefield have been painted well into the nineteenth century as well as up to the present day. This may be because it is one of the few cities in the region which can boast a distinctive and impressive sky-line when approached from the surrounding countryside. One such example is attributed to John Inigo Richards (c.1720-1810); it shows Wakefield at the turn of the nineteenth century and is taken from a high point, possibly Lowe, or Law Hill, which now forms part of Thornes Park. Richards' view is particularly interesting because the gathering of factual information – which had been the prime function of earlier topographers – has now given way to a more personal and aesthetic response to nature. Although the painting shows the Georgian developments in the city and the spire of the parish church as well as the tower of St John's church (completed 1794-95), the artist seems to be more taken by the dramatic sweep of landscape which leads the eye out over the city to the Aire valley in the distance.

The tradition of painting the prospect of Wakefield has continued into this century. F C Jones (1891-1956), a Bradford-born artist, was well known for his drawings of the towns and cities of Yorkshire. Wakefield is depicted as an industrial and urban area with numerous factory chimneys and a tightly built-up city centre in his watercolour entitled *View of Wakefield from Newton Hill* which was painted in 1945 (Figure 2). Yet at the same time the artist reveals how rural the immediate environs of Wakefield were even at this date. This pastoral feel is further enhanced by the horse and plough in the foreground and the dramatic sky which dwarfs the city's buildings. This picture was originally commissioned by the Wakefield Historical Society as a gift for their then president, J W Walker, author of *Wakefield – Its History and People*.

If we turn from all-encompassing artistic views of Wakefield to consider particular aspects of the city, it soon becomes apparent that the Chantry Chapel on Wakefield Bridge was considered to be Wakefield's jewel by visiting antiquaries and travellers. It was more frequently painted than any other local subject.

The chapel with its delicately carved facade was built in the middle of the fourteenth century as part of the medieval bridge with its nine pointed arches which spans the River Calder. Although praised by historians, the chapel was allowed to decay in the seventeenth and eighteenth centuries. It had gone out of use in 1548 following the Dissolution of Chantries, and was later let out for commercial purposes. A partial restoration in 1797 which repaired the front, replaced the blocked up windows with simpler ones and rebuilt the parapet on the north and south sides, was undertaken by the West Riding magistrates, who decided not to restore the building's beauty but to ensure its stability as it is structurally part of the bridge. *A perspective view of the chapel adjoining to Wakefield Bridge, in the County of York*, by George Fleming is the earliest surviving view

Figure 2. F C Jones, *View of Wakefield from Newton Hill*, 1945, watercolour. *Wakefield Art Gallery.*

Figure 3. George Fleming, *A Perspective View of the Chapel Adjoining Wakefield Bridge*, 1743, engraving. *Wakefield Art Gallery.*

of the chapel and dates from 1743 (Figure 3), but the chapel was most frequently painted in the eighteenth and early nineteenth centuries. This coincides with the period when gentlemen began to travel more in England to view both scenery and antiquities, often accompanied by a professional artist. At about the same time there was a proliferation of engraved views for books on travel and topography relating to the British Isles. This approach is exemplified by a pen, ink and wash drawing of the chapel by Samuel Hieronymus Grimm (1733-1794) dated 1778. Grimm by profession was a topographical watercolour painter and draughtsman. Born in Burgdorf, Switzerland, he settled in London in 1768. Grimm was an artist in great demand as a topographer by antiquaries, writers and travellers of the day. He was associated for over twenty years from 1773 with Dr Richard Kaye (1736-1809), an ecclesiastic and antiquarian who in 1783 became Dean of Lincoln. Grimm accompanied Kaye on his travels taking in the Midlands, the North, the South and West country. Along the way he produced a collection of drawings of landscape, social and architectural subjects which are now bound in twelve volumes in the collection of the British Museum. These drawings as a group represent one of the most important records of the appearance and manners of England in Grimm's day. It is possible that Grimm's view of the Chantry was drawn on or after a visit to Wakefield by the artist and Dr Kaye since another version of this drawing is in the Kaye collection held at the British Museum.

One of the most famous artists to visit Wakefield during this period was J M W Turner (1775-1851) who sketched the Chantry Chapel during his 1797 tour in the north of England and also produced a watercolour and an engraving of the subject. Turner's watercolour showing the south windows blocked up and the tracery almost gone, with later windows inserted, provides an interesting comparison with a similar view painted only four years earlier by Philip Reinagle (1749-1833) which draws a veil over the disrepair. Reinagle was born in Scotland, the son of a musician of Hungarian origin, and became a pupil of the court painter Allan Ramsay, whom he assisted with his portraits of George III and Queen Charlotte. Reinagle's *Wakefield Bridge and Chantry Chapel* is one of the most significant topographical views of the city and is certainly the most impressive scale wise (Figure 4). It was commissioned by James Milnes of Thornes House and it seems likely that Reinagle travelled up from London to sketch on site, producing the large-scale canvas on return to his London studio. Although on the whole topographically correct it is still a rather romanticized view of the subject – it certainly does not attempt to reveal the known ruinous state of the chapel as it was in 1793. This was done, obviously in part, to provide a pleasing view of the scene for the benefit of the artist's patron.

A smaller contemporary watercolour of the chapel's facade by Philip's son, Richard Ramsay Reinagle (1775-1862), unike the grander commission in oils, quite clearly shows the dilapidated condition of the building – particularly the damaged front and blocked windows.

A series of very detailed watercolours by John Buckler (1770-1851) and his son John Chessell Buckler (1793-1894) typify the

Figure 4. Phillip Reinagle, *View of Wakefield Bridge and Chantry Chapel. 1793*, oil. *Wakefield Art Gallery.*

nineteenth century fascination with architectural styles and record the state of the Chantry Chapel after restoration work in 1797 (Figure 5). The Bucklers also produced an extensive set of other local views for the Wakefield barrister Francis Maude in 1813. As a group these watercolours are probably the most detailed visual record of the city's architecture of the period. Born in Calbourne, Isle of Wight, Buckler senior practised in London as an architect until 1826. He is best known for his drawings of cathedrals, country houses and other notable buildings throughout the British Isles. Many of these images were later published as prints. The highly detailed and technical style of these drawings reveal Buckler's architectural training. He shows little interest in formal devices such as figures, trees and bushes with which to provide a more picturesque setting for the buildings.

In comparison to Buckler's architectural approach the pencil drawing of the *Chapel on Wakefield Bridge* dated 1825 by John Coney (1786-1833) is more fluid and compositionally dynamic (Figure 6). Coney drew and engraved an extensive series of views of English abbeys and cathedrals from 1815 to 1829 There are a number of original drawings of Yorkshire subjects by Coney held in Wakefield

Figure 5. John Chessell Buckler, *West Front of the Chapel on Wakefield Bridge*, 1813, watercolour. *Wakefield Art Gallery.*

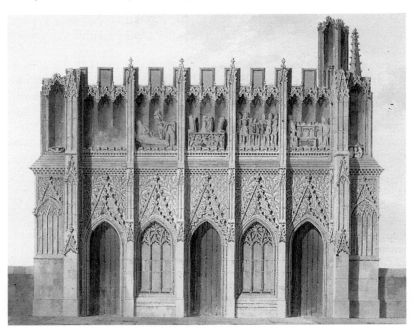

Art Gallery's Gott collection. This, made by John Gott (1830-1906) Vicar of Leeds and later Bishop of Truro, and his father William Gott (1797-1863) includes over 1,000 prints, watercolours, sketches and numerous maps and plans illustrative of the topography and architecture of the county of Yorkshire from c.1700 to c.1840.

By the second quarter of the nineteenth century the number of artistic images of the Chantry Chapel by notable artists were few and far between. It could be argued that this tailing off of interest was in part due to the restoration work of 1847-8 which led to the complete removal and relocation of the original facade. Also photography was to play an ever increasing role in the visual recording of architecture and historical monuments as the nineteenth century advanced.

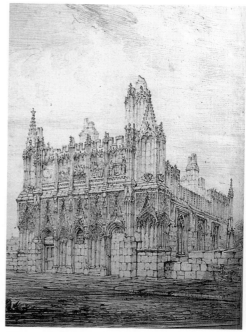

Figure 6. John Coney, *Chapel on Wakefield Bridge*, 1825, pencil.
Wakefield Art Gallery.

The centre of Wakefield itself had also attracted its fair share of artists, although fewer and less well known than those who came to record the Chantry. It is thanks to these individuals that Wakefield Art Gallery now has a comprehensive visual history of how the city and its architecture have changed, particularly from the late eighteenth century onwards.

Until comparatively recently Wakefield's distinctive sky-line has been dominated by the early fifteenth century spire of the parish church of All Saints which became Wakefield cathedral in 1888. Boasting the tallest spire in Yorkshire, the inclusion of this structure in artistic records of the city often cannot be avoided. Indeed after the Chantry it remains the city's most frequently painted landmark. Out of the twenty or so watercolours produced by John and John Chessell Buckler in 1813 for Francis Maude, at least five include at some point an aspect of this structure (Figure 7). Similarly the 1853 suite of lithographs produced by Reverend Thomas Kilby (1794-1868), arguably the most popular images of the city from the nineteenth century, includes numerous views of Wakefield with All

Saints and its imposing spire as an integral part of the composition. Although separated by only some forty years, the Buckler and Kilby images are poles apart in content and atmosphere. As trained architects it is not surprising that the Bucklers concentrate on depicting the fabric of Wakefield's most prominent buildings in some detail. In contrast Kilby's prints are more than topographical in nature since they are also full of figures and incident. These offer an insight into what life was like in Wakefield in 1853. You will find carriages driving around, fashionably dressed ladies and gentlemen, street urchins and even a shepherd driving a flock of sheep up Little Westgate (Figure 8).

This suite of fifteen lithographs is still much sought after locally because of its picturesque qualities. However it is worth remembering that these images were actually drawn by W Bevan for lithographic reproduction after original sketches by Kilby. This is quite clearly indicated on the prints themselves which have the inscription 'Rev'd T Kilby del. W Bevan -Lith.' An earlier set of views from 1843 entitled *Scenery in the Vicinity of Wakefield by an Amateur* was both drawn and reproduced by Kilby himself. There is quite a difference in quality and style between the two sets of images. The Kilby drawings of 1843 lack accomplishment and are very much the work of an amateur artist, whilst Bevan's interpretation of Kilby's 1853 scenes are highly accomplished and show the intervention of a master craftsman. As a professional lithographer, Bevan's livelihood was dependent on producing images of a high quality.

In 1865 Thomas Kilby, who was the vicar of St John's Church from 1825 to 1868, gained a second-class medal for pencil drawing

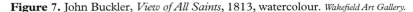

Figure 7. John Buckler, *View of All Saints*, 1813, watercolour. *Wakefield Art Gallery.*

Figure 8. Rev T Kilby, *South West View of the Parish Church from the Eastern Extremity of Westgate*, 1853, lithograph. *Wakefield Art Gallery.*

at the Wakefield Industrial and Fine Arts Exhibition behind Louisa Fennell (1847-1930). Fennell was Wakefield born and bred and her watercolours, produced at the turn of the century, sit alongside the work of Buckler and Kilby as being of great local importance. As a young lady amateur, Louisa Fennell turned to painting in 1860, studying under the Wakefield artist John Batty Tootal (c.1791-1865). She also trained at the Wakefield School of Art when it opened in 1866. For a period Fennell came under the influence of Thomas Hartley Cromek (1809-1873), a London born artist who spent much of his early life in Wakefield where he was also educated. From 1830 until 1849 he spent most of his time painting on the Continent, particularly in Italy and Greece.

Like Cromek, Fennell travelled extensively and painted views in Switzerland, Rome and Venice, but it is for her views of Wakefield that she is best remembered. These local images are at times compositionally naive, but they still provide much information about Wakefield and its buildings. For example she recorded the timber frame houses in Marygate just before their demolition when the road had to be widened in 1901 (Figure 9).

In 1907 two portfolios of eight prints were published by Goodall and Suddick, a Leeds printing company. These were direct reproductions of some of Fennell's original watercolours and the series was entitled *Views of Wakefield*. Although the colour quality of these prints has degraded somewhat over the years they are understandably still popular and many copies survive locally. Work after 1907 by Fennell is a rarity even though she lived to the ripe old age of eighty-four. She was buried in the churchyard of St John's Church, Wakefield, where her gravestone may still be seen.

By the end of the nineteenth century and certainly by the early part of this century we see the number of artists working in a strictly topographical manner diminishing greatly. This was in no small part due to the growing use of photography in the recording of buildings and places. It is almost certain that Fennell herself worked up her watercolours from photographs from time to time rather than sketching in situ.

Those artists who have maintained the topgraphical tradition have been able to do so because of their ability to successfully combine elements of traditional recording with their personal artistic style. Louis Grimshaw's (1870-1844) *View of Upper Westgate, Wakefield,* from 1896, is a moonlit scene very much in the style of his father Atkinson Grimshaw (1836-2893). This painting contains a number of the grand buildings erected along the top of Westgate in the nineteenth century, yet would have been very difficult to reproduce photographically given the camera technology of the period, because of its atmosphere of both artificial and natural light.

As the twentieth century advanced, artists became more confident in freeing themselves from the constraints of having to transcribe what they saw in a literal fashion. However, some were happy to uphold the more academic tradition. One such artist was Fred C Jones whose *View of Wakefield from Newton Hill* was mentioned earlier. Wakefield Art Gallery also houses other works by this artist including a view from the bottom of the Springs looking up to Wakefield Cathedral. Jones excelled in these records of the thriving urban centres of Yorkshire life and his close observational style reveals much interesting detail about the fashions of the day.

Another local artist from recent history who described himself as a topographer first and foremost was Joe Clay (1909-1997). Joe worked for the West Riding County Planning Department in Wakefield from 1944 until 1974. In the early 1960s he produced a

Figure 9. Louisa Fennell, *Marygate*, 1901. Watercolour *Wakefield Art Gallery.*

series of views of the city, all in ball-point pen, some with a touch of colour crayon, which were produced on the spot (Figure 10). However, in spite of his technical training he freely admitted that he did not look at things with a camera's eye, and Clay's drawings, whilst being faithful views retain a directness and charm which reflect the individuality of their creator.

One of the most interesting views of Wakefield to be produced in recent times is John McPake's etching *Wakefield in the Eighties* (Figure 11). This image shows how it is possible for modern artists

Figure 10. Joe Clay, *Upper Kirkgate from Wakefield Cathedral*, 1963.
Wakefield Art Gallery.

to mix successfully traditional descriptive elements with a knowledge
of contemporary artistic styles. The image was commissioned by the
Friends of Wakefield Art Gallery and Museums in 1985. McPake
was born in Barnsley in 1943 and first studied art at Wirral College
of Art. He also attended Liverpool, Birmingham and Leeds
Polytechnics and was, until 1996, the head of the Art Foundation
Course at Barnsley College. He currently lives at Thurlstone, near
Sheffield, and is a Fellow of the Royal Society of Painters, Etchers
and Engravers, a Fellow of the Printmakers Council and an associate
member of Yorkshire Printmakers. During the 1960s the society had
commissioned two paintings on a Wakefield subject by the artists
Druie Bowett (b.1924) and Peter Brook (b.1927), thus providing
much needed contemporary views of the city. It was decided to revive
this idea and commission a contemporary view from McPake. The
artist spent much time discovering Wakefield and produced
numerous sketches and photographic records of the city with the aim
of combining some of these observations in the final image. As
McPake says, ' I rarely transfer information directly...as this approach
can lead to reproduction rather than a creative exploitation of the
media. I prefer to synthesise one image with others...over a period of

time. In this way different apects of a house are combined; two rooms become an amalgamation; outside and inside are experienced simultaneously. The contemporary experience of the whole life, certainly for most of us I imagine in the developed West, must be very like this.'

This aesthetic approach is quite clearly expressed in McPake's etching *Wakefield in the Eighties* as it contains various composite views of the city's architecture old and new. Most notably, exterior views of the Ridings Shopping Centre are combined with an inverted view of the centre's interior glass and aluminium lift which provides the foreground and central vertical thrust to the design. However, even a contemporary artist like McPake cannot ignore those aspects of Wakefield which have fascinated visitors for centuries. In this most modern of image, the very top of the spire of Wakefield Cathedral makes an appearance, its tip just glimpsed above the rooftop of the shopping centre.

Figure 11. John McPake, *Wakefield in the Eighties*, 1985, etching. *Wakefield Art Gallery.*

Moreover, as if to come full circle, the Chantry Chapel and Wakefield Bridge are represented by the same view which so inspired Turner and Reinagle in the eighteenth century, and provides the central focus to one of the most recent images of Wakefield.

All the works referred to are in the collection of Wakefield Art Gallery

Bibliography
Wakefield Art Gallery, *Wakefield Through the Artist's Eye,* Exhibition Catalogue, 1975.
Wakefield Museum, *Louisa Fennell of Wakefield and her World 1847-1930,* Exhibition Catalogue, 1979.
Drawings of Wakefield by Joe Clay, Wakefield Historical Publications, 1984.
Wakefield Art Gallery, *John McPake – Etchings and Aquatints.* Exhibition Catalogue, 1986.
Wakefield Art Gallery, *Images of Wakefield and Beyond,* Exhibition Catalogue, 1989.

3. 'MY DRINK IS WATER BRIGHT': TEMPERANCE IN OSSETT 1848-1914

by David Scriven

FEW PEOPLE WHO BUY THEIR PET FOOD in Saga House in Ossett will have heard of the temperance movement. Yet Saga House was once the local centre of this national crusade to rid Britain of the 'curse' of alcohol. In what was then the temperance hall generations of children learned to sing that their drink was 'water bright' (Figure 1).

The first English temperance society was founded in Bradford in 1830 and its original members were moderationists; they believed that drinking in moderation was permissible. However, a more radical temperance movement started in Preston in 1832. This demanded total abstinence – teetotalism – and it became the most vigorous part of the temperance crusade. Its strength was in the dozens of local temperance societies, particularly in the north of England. The teetotalers did not ignore children. The Band of Hope, initiated in Leeds in 1847, became the most successful of temperance organisations for the young. Many members of the temperance movement were content to rely on moral persuasion to bring about their aim, but others argued that only through the legal prohibition of the sale of alcohol could a temperance reformation be brought

Figure 1. Ossett Temperance Hall. *Courtesy Ossett Historical Society.*

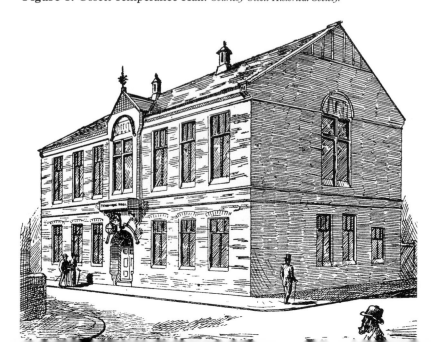

about. The United Kingdom Alliance, formed in 1853, became the organisation most closely associated with the prohibitionists. The Alliance made repeated attempts to persuade Parliament to introduce prohibition on a national or at a local level. The Liberals eventually included local prohibition, the local option, in their party programme, but the Conservative victory in the 1895 general election shattered the hopes of the prohibitionists. Not surprisingly it was impossible to maintain support for temperance at a high level and the movement experienced periods of growth and of decline. Its last great revival came in the 1880s when gospel temperance, a blend of temperance and religion imported from the United States, swept across the country.[1]

By the 1880s the temperance cause was well established in Ossett. The town's first temperance organisation, the Ossett Temperance and Mutual Improvement Society, was formed in 1848. It is possible that the impetus for its creation came from Wakefield as in March the advocates of temperance there were said to be 'very industrious in promoting their views'. The first members of the Ossett Temperance Society faced considerable popular prejudice. One later remembered that the 'scorn, ridicule and contempt' were almost 'unbearable'. In such circumstances teetotalers had to have strong characters. The story of Thomas Westwood, who moved to Ossett in the 1850s, gives an insight into their motives. Westwood's decision to take the pledge in 1839 seems to have been a reaction against his father's heavy drinking. This broke his health and plunged his family into poverty. At first his son took the pledge for three months at a time, partly because he was warned that his work as a miner was only possible with the help of beer. He found, however, that he worked better without it and became a lifetime teetotaler.[2]

The Ossett Temperance and Mutual Improvement Society provided its members with the support that teetotalers needed in a hostile environment. At first it took rooms in Little Town End, but it later moved to what became known as the Temperance Saloon – 'T'owd Saloon' – in Bank Street. Membership was initially 1d a week and later 5s a year. The Temperance Society seems to have had a vigorous existence for some twenty years, but in the 1870s it suffered a loss of membership with the formation of the town's Conservative and Liberal clubs. Eventually the old saloon became no more than a social club and admitted non-temperance members. This failed to stop its decline and in 1903 it closed. A Gawthorpe Temperance Society had an even shorter life. Formed in 1858, it disappeared from the pages of the local press after 1872.[3]

The decline of the Ossett Temperance Society left the town's Band of Hope Union as the most active exponent of temperance principles in the town. The Band of Hope seems to have made its first appearance in the town in 1861 or 1862 when the Gawthorpe Band of Hope was formed. Five years later supporters of the movement created the Ossett Coldstream Band of Hope. Their aim was to create Bands of Hope linked to the various places of worship in the town. However the number of Nonconformist denominations in Ossett made it difficult for this unsectarian organisation to work and as a result it was decided in 1870 to form sectarian Bands of Hope based on Sunday Schools. It was expected that these would affiliate to the Ossett Band of Hope Union. Some places of worship did form their own Bands but it is impossible to state how many because of lack of evidence. Press reports of the membership of the Ossett Band of Hope Union do, however, give us minimum numbers for the town's Bands of Hope for some years. Thus in 1876 the Union had two Ossett Bands affiliated to it, in 1879 eight, in 1885 thirteen, and in 1895 ten. To the disappointment of some temperance workers some Sunday schools seem never to have formed Bands of Hope. Speaking in 1879 J E Wilby criticised those ministers and Sunday school workers who gave temperance work the 'cold shoulder'. As is clear from the figures given above, the Ossett Band of Hope Union had a fluctuating membership. Yet it was successful enough to attract affiliates from nearby places. In 1894 these included Horbury, Netherton, Alverthorpe, Middlestown, Wrenthorpe and East Ardsley. The Union's membership was dominated by Nonconformist places of worship. Although both of Ossett's Anglican churches, Holy Trinity and Christ Church, were affiliated briefly in the 1870s, this Church of England presence was exceptional.[4]

The declining vigour of the Ossett Temperance Society encouraged the Band of Hope Union to extend its activities. From 1875 it organised temperance work not only among children but also among adults by holding public meetings and arranging lectures. Some Ossett teetotalers also joined the Good Templars, a temperance organisation of American origin. The Ossett Good Templars' Lodge was in existence by 1875 when it held a tea attended by 60 people, but judging by the lack of later references to it in the local press it was short lived. Its work with adults was soon supplemented by that of the Ossett Gospel Temperance Missionary Society formed in 1881 with the Reverend J P Perkins, minister of the Green Congregational Church, as its president. The Society at once organised a successful mission in Ossett which garnered 400-

500 pledges. It was possibly the formation of the Gospel Temperance Missionary Society which encouraged Canon Addison, the vicar of Holy Trinity, to form a branch of the Church of England Temperance Society in 1882. Neither society, however, seems to have survived long as both soon vanished from the local press. More durable was the Salvation Army, an organisation advocating temperance, which in 1885 purchased a former Wesleyan Methodist chapel in Gawthorpe as its Ossett headquarters. The impact of the Salvation Army was lessened because it was unable to attract large-scale support in the town: a count of local households' religious affiliations carried out in 1894 showed only 11 families associated with the Salvation Army.[5]

All of the older adult temperance organisations in the town were overshadowed when in 1884 the Ossett Temperance Society and Alliance Auxiliary was formed. This new organisation, which was to dominate temperance work in the town until 1914, originated from a reunion of the town's veteran teetotalers at 'a good old fashioned teetotal tea' held in the Assembly Rooms on the Green. The aims of the Society were to influence public opinion in Ossett in favour of temperance legislation, to prepare schemes for the reclamation of drunkards and to confirm in their principles those already pledged. The Society was not welcomed by all of Ossett's temperance workers. Among those who could not support it was the Reverend J P Perkins. As a moral suasionist he opposed the link between the Society and the Alliance. He felt that it would have been wiser to have kept the Society and the Alliance Auxiliary quite separate.[6]

The Reverend Perkins' opposition was fruitless. The new Society quickly showed its vigour by building the town's first temperance hall. Although the old Temperance Society had purchased land in West Wells in 1866 to build such a hall, it had never raised sufficient funds to put its intentions into effect. In 1887 the trustees of the land exchanged it with the Local Board of Health for a plot at the corner of Illingworth Street and Prospect Road. It was there that the new Society opened its hall in 1888. Mr W A Kendall, the architect, designed the outside of the hall in the '17th century style modernised', while inside he provided a main room seating 470 people with an additional 80 in its gallery. Part of the cost of more than £1,500 was met by borrowing, but the Society was able to clear the debt within three years.[7]

The new Society tried to fulfil its aims by holding indoor and outdoor meetings and it also began to hold Sunday services in the new hall. Yet by 1901 one Ossett temperance worker was beginning to feel 'disheartened and discouraged' . However a new impetus was given to the Society's work in that year when it appointed John Roberts as its first full-time agent. Roberts, who was assisted by his equally active wife, brought a new enthusiasm to temperance work in the town. In 1903 Mrs Roberts took over from her husband as agent because he was devoting more time to temperance work outside Ossett. Following the departure of Mr and Mrs Roberts for Leicester in 1905 the Society decided to continue using an agent. Mr Isaac Wilkinson was appointed to the post and, helped by his wife, filled it until his death in 1910. He was then replaced by Mr J W Booth.[8]

The leadership of all the temperance organisations discussed so far was male. Women were, however, members of both the old and the new Temperance Societies. Thus in 1864 20 of the old Society's 77 members were women. Their contribution to temperance work was only rarely publicly remarked on by the officials of their societies. An exception was in 1910 when at the annual meeting of the new Temperance Society the secretary commented that without the help of the 'ladies' the Society would have been in great difficulties. He went on to note that,

> *Whenever in the committee meetings it was suggested that the women should do this thing or that, it was always carried unanimously by the men.*[9]

Ossett did have one temperance organisation specifically for women. This was the Women's Christian Temperance Union which was formed in 1891. At its inaugural meeting in the Temperance Hall the platform was, in the words of the local newspaper, 'filled with ladies' who 'fairly surprised many persons in the audience by their ability as public speakers'. All of the speakers advocated teetotalism as the antidote to intemperance and stressed the powerful influence that women could wield. At a later meeting Mrs G H Hinchcliffe explained the nature of this influence. The Union did not, she said, want to take women away from their homes, but to persuade them to make their home so comfortable that their men would not leave them at night for public houses. By 1896 the Union had a membership of 136 but it then disappears from the local press.[10]

Membership figures for the town's other temperance organisations are available for some years, but they are too few to trace the fluctuating fortunes of the temperance movement with any precision. At its peak the old Temperance Society is said to have had a membership of 'several hundreds'. Certainly at its third annual soiree in 1851 more than 300 people sat down to tea. By 1864 its membership had fallen to 77 and in 1873 it had only 'about 50' members. The new Temperance Society had 117 members in 1884, but later newspaper reports of its activities fail to give the size of its membership. The numbers involved in adult temperance organisations were dwarfed by those of the Ossett Coldstream Guard Band of Hope: in 1868 it had 780 children in its ranks. The Band of Hope Union, which included Bands from outside the town, also had a large membership in some years. A recruiting drive brought it up to 1,600 in 1892. Unfortunately it is impossible to say how many of those who took the pledge as a result of such campaigns remained teetotalers. Eli Townend, one of Ossett's most successful businessmen, was a teetotaler until he was 35. After that he was, in his own words, teetotal 'in principle, lacking only in practice.' On the other hand there were those who, having taken the pledge, kept it. Some 180 people attended a celebration dinner in the Temperance Hall in 1898 when Jack Rhodes and Thomas Whitehead completed 50 years of total abstinence. The speeches after the dinner revealed that teetotalism sometimes ran in families. Bennett Brook, for example, was proud to claim that his children, grandchildren and great-grandchildren were teetotalers.[11]

Ossett's temperance organisations employed a variety of methods to spread their message. One used very often was the indoor or outdoor public meeting. Outdoor meetings were often held in the Market Place in the centre of the town, but they were also staged in other parts of Ossett such as Ossett Common and Gawthorpe. A disadvantage of the outdoor meeting was the opportunity it gave to opponents of temperance to make their views known. When in 1902 John Roberts condemned the drinking which had marred the town's celebration of the end of the South African War, he aroused so much hostility that the police had to escort him from the meeting in the Market Place. Indoor meetings were much less likely to be interrupted, but until the opening of the Temperance Hall in 1888, the local temperance movement had to rely on churches and chapels to provide accommodation.

Mr Troughton's temperance mission in 1880 made use of rooms belonging to the Congregationalists at the Green, Gawthorpe and Flushdyke and the Primitive Methodists at Ossett Common. Even after the opening of the Temperance Hall meetings were sometimes held in other premises. When the social investigator Joseph Rowntree visited Ossett in 1899 to outline his proposals for the public control of the drinks trade, the conference he addressed was held in the Methodist Free Church. At most meetings the speaker was content to rely on the power of his words. Some were very successful: Mr Inwards 'riveted the attention of the audience for an hour and forty minutes' when he spoke to the old Temperance Society in 1853. Occasionally, however, speakers made use of visual aids. Lantern slides were used by Mr A Houldershaw in 1894 to illustrate his talk on 'Alcohol and its relation to the blood and infectious diseases.'[12]

The temperance message was also spread by the distribution of tracts (Figure 2). Members of the new Temperance Society distributed 2,000 copies of *Bank Holiday in Blackpool* and 1,000 copies of *The Socialists' Propaganda and the Drink Question* in 1893-4. Such pamphlets were the products of a flourishing temperance publishing industry which supplied societies up and down the country.[13]

House to house visits were another method of winning and retaining support for temperance. Such visits were a regular part of the work of the agents of the new Temperance Society: in one year Mrs Roberts made 1,200 home visits. Perhaps the most thorough visitation of the town took place in 1891 as part of the United Kingdom Band of Hope Union's attempt to win one million more members. The 70 volunteers who carried out these visits were able to obtain 677 new pledges from children in the Ossett area.[14]

The Bands of Hope were an important part of the town's temperance culture. Addressing the Wesleyan Band of Hope in 1875, the Reverend J P Perkins claimed that

> *No branch of temperance work was....so important as their Band of Hope...A far surer way of lessening the evils of drunkenness than by Acts of Parliament was the impartation of sound instruction to their young people, and the spread of total abstinence principles among them.*

Not surprisingly one of the most active Bands of Hope in the town was that of Perkins' own chapel, the Green Congregational Chapel. Its annual report for 1881-2 showed a rise in membership from 65 to 150. There had been 43 meetings, seven speeches given by the children and two temperance sermons given by their minister. Censuses of the town's public houses and of its places of worship were carried out during the year by the Band of Hope's young men.[15]

Not all of the town's children attended Bands of Hope and so temperance workers tried to gain access to Sunday and day schools. At the annual meeting of the Band of Hope Union in 1880 it was reported that nearly all of the Sunday schools in the district had been asked to allow a temperance address to be given once a quarter and that only one school had refused permission. Day schools were visited less frequently, but in 1882 William Bell, who was carrying out a week's temperance mission, gave talks in Christ Church and Trinity schools and the Grammar School. Temperance workers were not, however, always welcome in day schools. A change of vicar at Christ Church led to a change of policy towards temperance

Figure 2. Ossett's temperance organisations frequently distributed tracts in the hope of winning converts. This particular tract tells the story of how one drinker was almost brought to destruction in the Queen's Vaults but turned to teetotalism at the last moment. The illustrations reinforce the story by vividly showing the consequences of drunkenness.

OSSETT & DISTRICT BAND OF HOPE UNION
NEW YEAR'S TRACT.

"The Queen's Vaults"; or, "The Caverns of the Damned."
By GUY HAYLER.

THERE have been many ways in which men and women addicted to drinking have been led to see their error and induced to sign the teetotal pledge. "Buy your own cherries," said by a publican's wife to a regular customer about to pick a cherry from a basket-full standing on the counter, not only resulted in the drunkard becoming a teetotaler, a respectable member of society, and a blessing to his family, but by the incident

No. 279.

lectures. In 1894 the Reverend John Kirk refused permission for a temperance talk to be given in the church school by a representative of the United Kingdom Band of Hope Union. He argued that it would be wrong to subject the children to a 'scientific controversy' over the merits of drink and that he was behaving fairly as he would not have allowed a lecturer from the licensed victuallers to speak to the children.[16]

Local temperance workers were well aware of the value of the town's newspaper, the *Ossett Observer*, in publicising their views: the Reverend Kirk was attacked, and defended himself, in the correspondence columns. During the following year temperance workers again resorted to the press when a local publican was granted an occasional licence to sell wine at a public luncheon at Holy Trinity school bazaar. One former Ossett resident hinted 'I know something of past unfortunate events of this kind in connection with this church and school', while another correspondent wrote that within three miles of his own house one Congregational minister, one Primitive Methodist minister and one Church of England minister had recently become victims of the 'arch-demon drink'. In addition to opening its correspondence column to the temperance debate, the *Ossett Observer* also publicised the movement by giving full accounts of the activities of the various temperance organisations in the town. There were, of course, good commercial reasons for this, but Stephen Cockburn, who became owner and editor of the *Observer* in 1873 was himself a temperance advocate. It was Cockburn who in 1882 proposed the motion to form a Church of England Temperance Society in the town.[17]

The Ossett temperance organisations were eager not only to convert individuals to their cause, but also to restrict the opportunities for those who wanted to drink. One method was to oppose the granting of licences at the annual brewster sessions held by the local magistrates. On such occasions a solicitor was engaged to argue the temperance case before the magistrates and petitions against the objectionable applications were submitted to the court. As the brewster sessions were not concerned with the rights and wrongs of teetotalism, the temperance case was usually that Ossett had more than enough on and off licences. Opposition to the granting of licences was not always successful, but on some occasions the temperance movement did get its way. Thus in 1894, following a vigorous campaign, the magistrates refused to grant a licence to a new public house called the *Empress* which was stigmatised by its opponents as an 'additional moral and social pestilence'. By 1903 the

Ossett magistrates had been convinced that the town had too many licensed premises and during the next eleven years the number of public houses dropped by one. In 1914 the town had 34 taverns, a rise of only two since 1870.[18]

From time to time there were complaints from teetotalers about the number of drunks in Ossett. It was the task of the police to enforce the law against drunkenness and in 1873-4 the officer in charge of the Ossett station, Sergeant Helliwell, became the centre of controversy over his allegedly unduly strict interpretation of the law. Helliwell's membership of the Independent Order of Good Templars was said by his opponents to be the reason for his severity. The sergeant's activities created such popular resentment in the town that the police constables were turned out of their lodgings and had to take shelter in the police station. The Local Board of Health took up the matter and persuaded the Chief Constable, Captain McNeil, to hold an inquiry into the sergeant's conduct. When McNeil's inquiry failed to condemn the sergeant, the Local Board complained, with no apparent success, to the Home Office. What perhaps particularly angered the Local Board in this case was that among Helliwell's victims were a number of local tradesmen who were 'fresh' rather than drunk. Although the episode was seized on by opponents of the temperance cause, it seems to have done little or no harm to the movement in Ossett. The two men who polled the highest in the Local Board elections in 1874 were both known as temperance men and one of them, Henry Westwood, was a Good Templar.[19]

Teetotalers inevitably became involved in local government and candidates for the Board of Highway Surveyors and then its successor, the Local Board of Health, were nominated at the Old Saloon. Members of the old Temperance Society canvassed for their candidates and when they were successful they sometimes celebrated at the Saloon. Temperance itself does not seem to have been an issue in local elections, although after 1893, when the new Borough of Ossett gained its own bench of magistrates, drawn in part from the council, the temperance movement had a motive to see more teetotalers elected as councillors. Certainly in the 1894 municipal election William Horsnell was referred to as the 'teetotal candidate'. Conversely the temperance movement wanted to keep publicans off the borough council. In 1903 J H Roberts condemned the Ossett and Horbury Trades Council for supporting the candidature of a miner who was also a publican. Eight years later the supporters of T W Bentley, an advocate of educational improvement, thought that votes could be won with a poster reading, 'What! Are you going to vote for Redgwick, the publicans' candidate? Not likely. Then vote for Bentley, the children's friend.' Some of the temperance men elected to local office came to play an important part in the town's public life. At least seven of the seventeen men who served as mayor between 1890 and 1914 had links with the temperance movement.[20]

Among the town's temperance community there were those who were anxious to see Parliament take action against drink. They therefore tried to mobilise opinion in support of parliamentary measures such as the local option by holding meetings and petitioning Parliament. In 1881 for example a 200 signature petition in favour of Sunday closing was sent from the Methodists of Wesley Street to W H Leatham, one of the local Liberal M Ps. Naturally the local temperance movement also tried to mobilise opinion against parliamentary measures it disliked. The 1904 Licensing Bill was bitterly opposed in Ossett because it contained proposals for compensating publicans whose licences were suppressed. An Anti-Licensing Committee was formed with delegates from the Nonconformist churches, the Sunday School Union, the Free Church Council, the Wesley Guild, the Temperance Society and the Band of Hope Union. The Ossett magistrates added their support to the movement and the mayor chaired a ratepayers' meeting which unanimously condemned the Licensing Bill. The measure was, however, passed by Parliament.[21]

This reverse highlighted what the temperance lobby had long known – the importance of having M Ps who were pledged to its cause. This could be achieved only for those parliamentary candidates who favoured it. To encourage Ossett voters to do this there was an unsuccessful attempt to form a Temperance Electoral Association early in 1885. The temperance question was, however, raised at election meetings in the town later in the year and the Liberal candidate, Charles Milnes-Gaskell, won the approval of one of the leading temperance workers in the town, William Horsnell. Seven years later, during the 1892 general election, the new Temperance Society submitted a list of questions concerning the local veto and Sunday closing to the two candidates for the local constituency. On the basis of the answers received, the Society then issued a leaflet urging temperance men to vote for the Liberal candidate, Mr Hutton, who was returned. At the next general election in 1895 the new Temperance Society again supported Hutton and he was again victorious. Nationally, however, the Liberals were defeated. Some Liberals blamed this reverse on their party's support for the United Kingdom Alliance's policy of the local veto. Among these Liberals was the Reverend J P Perkins, formerly minister of the Green Congregational Chapel. Perkins became engaged in a heated public correspondence with Henry Hibbert, the Bradford agent of the Alliance, about the cause of the Liberal defeat. Perkins accused the Alliance of being an organisation for 'crippling, harrying and splitting the great Liberal party' by urging the local veto on it, while Hibbert argued that the opposition of the brewers to the local veto showed that it was a practical policy.

Controversies such as this convinced some temperance activists that a temperance party was needed. Among them was John Roberts, the radical agent of Ossett's Temperance Society, who wrote to the *Ossett Observer* in 1904 announcing the formation of the National Independent Temperance Party. In spite of Roberts' links with the town, no branch of the new party was formed in Ossett. One critic of the scheme commented that it would alienate all true friends of the cause and that concentration on absolute teetotalism had done more damage to the temperance movement than anything else.[22]

For many in the temperance movement their work was a religious crusade based on supposed biblical prohibitions of wine drinking. J H Roberts even argued that teetotalism should be a condition of membership of any Christian church. Given such ideas it is not surprising that the new Temperance Society began to hold its own religious services on Sunday evenings in the Temperance Hall. How popular these services were is difficult to discover. The reports of the annual meetings of the new Temperance Society do not give figures for attendance, confining themselves to statements such as that services were growing in popularity or that there was room for improvement in attendance. Some figures are provided, however, by a survey of the religious affiliations of 1,838 Ossett households carried out in 1894. This reveals that only five households attended the services at the Temperance Hall, the smallest number of any place of worship in Ossett.[23]

Both the old and new Temperance Societies became centres of social activities intended, at least in part, to provide an alternative to the public houses. The rooms of the old Temperance Society in Bank Street, the Old Saloon, were a meeting place where members could talk, read the newspapers and borrow books from a small library. At first no games were provided but later whist, draughts, chess and bagatelle were introduced. Members of the Society also formed their own band, the Ossett Temperance Brass Band, which provided entertainment at temperance events. Eventually the social events of the old Temperance Society became the main reason for its existence with the result that the new Temperance Society was formed in 1884.[24]

Although the new Temperance Society never allowed its social role to dominate its missionary work, it did provide a variety of activities. From its early years it had its own debating society and after 1901, thanks partly to the energies of its full-time agents, it provided Saturday concerts, Pleasant Monday Evenings, women's at homes, a Christian Social Union and cricket and football teams. A gymnasium was built for members in 1906, but this was not a success. It was therefore converted into a billiards room and this was much more popular. There were, however, some doubts about the propriety of the Temperance Society promoting billards: Herbert Smith, the Society's president, hinted that there were more suitable ways for young men to 'better themselves physically, mentally and spiritually'.[25]

From the first the Bands of Hope also offered their members social activities. Thus at the first anniversary meeting of the Ossett Coldstream Guard Band of Hope it was reported that a drum and fife band and a singing class had been started. After the reorganisation of the Bands of Hope on sectarian lines such activities continued. Concerts involving chldren were common and sometimes on an ambitious scale: in 1895 the Green Congregational Band of Hope's performance of the cantata 'Agatha' involved 150 performers. For many children the annual summer festival of the Band of Hope Union was no doubt the highlight of the temperance calendar. The format of the occasion remained very much the same year after year: a procession of Bands of Hope through the town to a field where there were tea, speeches, sports and entertainment. In 1892, for example, the Bands of Hope went in procession from the Market Place to the football field near the town railway station. There they had tea and took part in sports and a grand concert, while later one Band of Hope did maypole plaiting and another gave a display of Japanese fan drill. Parents were able to admire an exhibition of the writing, drawing and sewing of Band of Hope children and additional entertainment was provided by bands from Ossett and Horbury and gymnasts from the Leeds YMCA.[26]

The attempts of the various temperance organisations to provide leisure activities to compete with those offered by public houses were supplemented by entrepreneurs who saw that profits might be made catering for the temperance market. One such businessman was Charles Hallgarth who in 1879 opened the Temperance Cocoa

House in Dearden Street to provide a place for people to meet without having to call for beer. Hall soon expanded the facilities of his Cocoa House by adding a concert room, the opening of which was celebrated with a tea attended by between 30 and 40 young men. The *Ossett Observer* commented that his 'hale and hearty appearance' did credit to his 'dietetic principles'. Hallgarth did not remain long at the Cocoa House, which was advertised to let in 1886, but moved to Bank Street where he became the proprietor of the Temperance Hotel.[27]

In October 1901 the president of the Ossett Temperance Society and Alliance Auxiliary, Councillor Horsnell, claimed that he was as certain that the temperance cause would triumph as he was that the sun would shine the following day. With the benefit of hindsight we know that his confidence was misplaced. Yet this does not mean that the crusade against drink in the town was misplaced. Teetotalism certainly remained a minority creed, but there were sufficient converts to it to support over the years a variety of temperance organisations,. These, however, were sometimes short lived. Even the more durable institutions, the Bands of Hope and the old and new Temperance Societies, had fluctuating support. However the derision which greeted teetotalism in some quarters in Ossett in the 1830s and the 1840s seems to have died by 1914. The number of public houses in the town had also stabilised and the borough's magistrates had been won over to the view that Ossett had too many inns. The two temperance societies and the Bands of Hope had also provided their members with a variety of social activities as alternatives to the public house. The new Temperance Society looked after the religious needs of its members by organising Sunday services, while their savings were cared for by a teetotal friendly society, the Independent Order of Rechabites. Temperance activists were able to find satisfaction in the roles of secretary, treasurer, president or committee member of one or other of the local organisations. Such work was valuable training for those who later entered local government, sometimes with the aid of the members of the Old Saloon.[28]

In many ways the history of the temperance movement in Ossett mirrored the national history of the temperance crusade. The 1830s and 1840s were a time of growth for the movement and it was in 1848 that the old Temperance Society was founded, while by the 1870s the movement was in recession and the old Temperance Society was losing vigour. Gospel temperance helped to revive the movement in the 1880s and in Ossett the new Temperance Society

was formed. Nationally teetotalers began to create an alternative
culture with its own drink-free institutions, and in Ossett the new
Temperance Society catered for its members' religious and leisure
needs.[29]

The records of the temperance organisations discussed in this
essay have not survived and so their activities have been
reconstructed from local newspapers.

Notes and References

1. Two modern accounts of the temperance movement are Lilian Lewis
Sharman, Crusade against *Drink in Victorian England* (London, 1988) and
Brian Harrison, *Drink and the Victorians,* second edition (London, 1994).
2. *Ossett Observer,* 2.5.1903 ; 28.12.1912; *Wakefield Journal,* 3.3.1848;
Ossett Observer, 23.2.1884.
3. *Ossett Observer,* 2.5.1903; 28.12.1912; *Wakefield Express,* 30.5.1858.
4. *Ossett Observer,* 10.11.1866; 23.3.1867; 2.4.1870; 4.3.1876; 9.8.1879;
21.2.1885; 16.3.1895; 4.3.1882; 21.7.1894; 1.11.1879.
5. *Ossett Observer,* 4.3.1876; 30.10.1875; 30.7.1881; 15.10.1881; 11.2.1882;
22.8.1885; 3.2.1894.
6. *Ossett Observer,* 23.2.1884; 1.3.1884; 29.3.1884.
7. *Ossett Observer,* 14.11.1885; 10.12.1887; 3.12.1898; 1.9.1888; *Wakefield
Express,* 17.1.1891.
8. *Ossett Observer,* 3.6.1905; 20.10.1906; 15.10.1910; 25.10.1913.
9. *Wakefield Express,* 12.6.1864; *Ossett Observer,* 15.10.1910.
10. *Ossett Observer,* 26.12.1891; 11.2.1893; 15.2.1896.
11. *Ossett Observer,* 28.12.1912; *Wakefield Express,* 12.2.1864; *Ossett
Observer,* 5.4.1873; 18.10.1884; 28.3.1868; 12.3.1892; 22.10.1910
(Townend's obituary); 17.12.1898.
12. *Ossett Observer,* 14.7.1902; 6.11.1880; 7.10.1899; *Wakefield Express,*
12.2.1853; *Ossett Obsever,* 22.12.1894.
13. *Ossett Observer,* 13.10.1894.
14. *Wakefield Express,* 17.10.1903; 17.10.1891; *Ossett Observer,* 12.3.1892.
15. *Ossett Observer,* 4.12.1875; 22.4.1882.
16. *Ossett Observer,* 13.3.1880; 22.7.1882; 1.12.1894; 8.12.1894;
15.12.1894.
17. *Ossett Observer,* 23.2.1895; 2.3.1895; 11.1.1882
18. *Ossett Observer,* 13.10.1894; 14.2.1903; 15.1.1870; 14.2.1914.
19. *Wakefield Free Press,* 3.1.1874; 24.1.1874; *Wakefield Express,*
3.1.1874; 17.1.1874; 9.5.1874; 23.5.1874.
20. *Ossett Observer,* 2.5.1903; 28.12.1912; 7.4.1877; 3.2.1872;
10.11.1894; 24.10.1903; 31.10.1903; 7.11.1908.
21. *Ossett Observer,* 9.7.1881; 14.5.1904; 4.6.1904.
22. *Ossett Observer,* 7.3.1885; 18.4.1885; 31.10.1885; 28.11.1885;
15.10.1892; 3.9.1904; 2.7.1904.
23. *Ossett Observer,* 8.2.1902; 3.2.1894.
24. *Ossett Observer,* 2.5.1903; 28.12.1912; *Wakefield Express,* 9.2.1856.
25. *Ossett Observer,* 19.10.1901; 20.10.1906; 16.10.1909.
26. *Ossett Observer,* 28.3.1868; 30.3.1895; 16.7.1892.
27. *Ossett Obsever,* 13.9.1879; 10.1.1880; 13.3.1880; 13.2.1886; *Kelly's Directory of the West Riding
of Yorkshire, 1889,* London (1888), p.985; *Kelly's Directory of the West Riding
of Yorkshire,* 1908, London (1907), p.693.
28. *Ossett Observer,* 19.10.1901; 20.1.1886: Rechabites.
29. This alternative culture does not seem to have been as well developed as in nearby Birstall: see
Lilian L Shiman, 'The Birstall Temperance Society', *Yorkshire Archaeological Journal,* 46 (1974).

4. BRAMWELL ARTHUR PASHLEY AND 'PEGGY TUB MAIN'

by Keith Wainwright

IF ONE INDUSTRY WAS TO STAND ALOOF from the others in the field of instinctive invention, that distinction would surely be accorded to the mining industry.

It was the major advances in mining technology in the nineteenth century which had led to the local dominance of the industry during the ensuing revolution in industrial achievement. Coal was nature's gift to the communities which were at that time expanding in the immediate area around Wakefield. It was a commodity which, with a reasonable amount of capital tempered with a certain degree of luck, might be expected to provide a healthy return on financial outlay. Crigglestone, four miles to the south-west of Wakefield, could be described as such a populace and expansion in the local coalfield by Joseph Charlesworth, John Moore and David Kaye amongst others had led to the existence of over twenty working mines in the parish by the mid 1860s.[1]

The workforce for these mines was always readily available, wages being a little more lucrative when compared with the meagre income of the other major provider of employment, agriculture. Many families were to rely on the ready work it provided as their foremost means of support. Many took the work without hesitation; indeed it was not uncommon to find three generations from one family working in the mines simultaneously. Others, however, could not adapt to the alien environment, more often than not returning readily to their former occupation.

Today many of the families who were instrumental in the development of the industry in the parish are still represented locally in their descendants.[2] Individuals from these families were occasionally gifted with the inventive qualities bestowed on their forefathers. One such was Bramwell Arthur Pashley, whose qualities in mining invention and improvisation were destined to make him a national celebrity.

'Bram' Pashley was born one of a family of four at Woodmoor, Newmillerdam, in 1906. His father and his grandfather had both been active locally in the mining industry and Bram's passion to

PLAN
of
workings in the
WOODMOOR SEAM
at
WOODMOOR COLLIERY
NEWMILLERDAM.

Abandoned January 1927

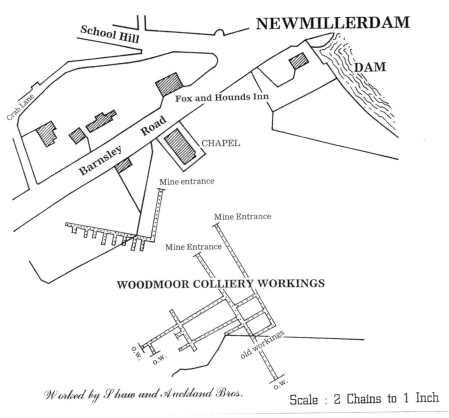

Figure 1. Woodmoor Colliery, Newmillerdam. Abandoned due to flooding in 1927. *Keith Wainwright.*

continue in the same vein was nurtured from a very early age. He was a boy who was gifted with an alert and active mind and was always sketching or drawing, his subjects usually being of a mining or mining-related nature. The industry intrigued him and his interest in it grew with his age. He dreamed of the day when he would own and manage his own colliery.

In 1919 Bram put his schooldays at Newmillerdam behind him and, as might be anticipated, took up employment in the local Woodmoor Colliery of Shaw and Auckland Brothers, situated near the Wesleyan Chapel at lakeside, Newmillerdam (Figure 1).[3]

For a time the small colliery expanded. Working conditions in the Woodmoor seam worked there were never amenable, however, and in 1926 a heading being worked in the seam broached an area of waterlogged old workings, the inrush causing severe flooding.[4] The ensuing miners' strike ended any chance of pumping the mine dry and the little pit was abandoned in January 1927.

Disillusioned by the miners' strike and the subsequent short-time working, Bram opted to divert his endeavours to other directions. In partnership with his brother Alf, he acquired a lorry and put it to use delivering an assortment of materials from Wakefield to the Lancashire area though trips to London, the Midlands and even Brighton were not uncommon.[5] By 1931 the Pashley brothers' business activities were to be expended more locally, leading coal from the pit head to factory and home alike.

A tragic road accident at Sandal which claimed the life of Alf Pashley in 1934 heralded a sombre winding up of the haulage business.

The nagging desire to own and manage his own colliery was never far from Bram's thoughts and a keenness to be involved in some form or other in the mining industry saw him take up employment as a mechanic at nearby Benzol and By-Products Ltd colliery at Crigglestone.

In 1938 Bram's father in law, Arthur Scorah, erected a pair of semi-detached houses adjacent to Denby Dale Road at Calder Grove, the Pashleys and Scorahs taking up residence there before the year's end. A lifelong interest in mining locally had included much research into old records and plans. This had convinced Bram that beneath the area surrounding his new home and at a shallow depth, a coal seam of not inconsiderable value was intact and awaiting exploitation. He had calculated that the seam – the Top Beamshaw seam – lay at a depth of some twenty-four feet beneath his property. In support of his conviction, he purchased the adjoining area of land.

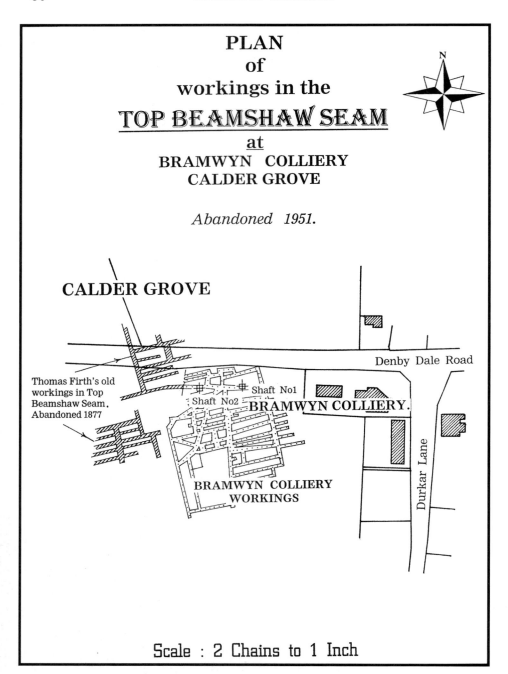

Figure 2. Bramwyn ('Peggy Tub Main') Colliery, Calder Grove. Abandoned due to flooding in 1951. *Keith Wainwright.*

This would ultimately form the site of his childhood dream, his own colliery, Bramwyn No 1 (Figure 2).

Retaining his full-time employment at Crigglestone Colliery, Bram began excavating his first shaft in his spare time.[6] His inventive aptitude was soon to be tested and his mother-in-law was the one to suffer, though not for the last time! She was coaxed into parting with her mangle, which was adapted and put to use as a winch over the proposed shaft, and her peggy tub, which Bram adapted and utilised as a means of removing spoil from the shaft excavation.[7]

The Calder Grovers, never slow to air their wit, followed Bram's progress with more than a passing interest. They re-named the little pit in their village 'Peggy Tub Main'. It was a named destined to survive the life of the colliery.

Work on the five-foot square shaft sinking made steady progress over the months ahead, timber shoring being used to support the unstable vertical shaft sides.[8] In early 1945 the Top Beamshaw seam was penetrated at a depth of twenty-six feet from the surface.[9] Bram had been a mere two feet out in his calculations. His other prognosis was also confirmed – there were no signs of previous workings. There was a bonus, too, the seam having a thickness of forty-three inches, six inches thicker than had been anticipated. His confidence in his

Figure 3. 'Peggy Tub Main' in full production, May 1949.

enterprise appears to have been fully vindicated.

In November 1945, 5,500 second-hand bricks were delivered to the site.[10] These were to be utilised in replacing the timber shoring temporarily supporting the shaft sides of Peggy Tub Main. 'They were all second-hand, different in size and all had to be cleaned. I had never laid a brick in my life, but I can now,' Bram remarked to a newspaper reporter at the time.

With the installation of the shaft lining began the replacement of the temporary winch. In its place was erected a timber headgear rising some twenty feet above ground level.[11] (Figure 3). An Austin Seven car wheel took its proud position as winding wheel atop the timber frame. A timber and steel cage slung within the headgear provided a means of haulage for future coal extraction. Power for the winder was provided by a converted Austin Seven engine unit (Figure 4).

The first shaft completed, work commenced immediately on the mandatory second shaft sinking.[12] This would provide an alternative means of access to and escape from the workings if need arose. The second shaft would also complete the ventilation circuit, causing the dissipation of any mine gas encountered below ground.

As a temporary means of ventilating his first drivage heading, Bram, ever the resourceful, appropriated, adapted and installed his

Figure 4. 'Peggy Tub Main' with a part of the Austin Seven car. *The John Goodchild Collection.*

wife's vacuum cleaner, only returning it when the roadway had broken through to his second shaft and completed his ventilation circuit.[13]

For a working licence to be granted to a colliery, the law required the employment of a deputy. Bram held a deputy's certificate but knew that at times he would be unavoidably away from the mine, unable to carry out his legal underground duties. To allow for any unforseen problems which might arise, he knew it was in his best interests to employ a dependable replacement. This was to be Jack Hutchinson of Kirkgate, Wakefield, who took up his responsibilities on 5 January 1948 when the licence to commence production was officially approved.[14] The other five miners employed at the colliery included Bram's seventy-three year old father, William.[15]

Nationalisation of the mining industry became a reality in January 1947. At that time about 480 of the 1,400 mines in the country were classified as 'small mines', perhaps employing as few as half a dozen men. In the case of the larger of these mines, the plant and equipment as well as the mines themselves were to become vested in the National Coal Board under the *Act of Nationalisation*. The remaining mines – and Peggy Tub Main was among these – were considered too small to be included in the new state-owned industry and were invited to apply for individual working licences before commencing coal production.

All Bram's employees enjoyed the concessions granted to other miners, awarded when Nationalisation of the industry took place.[16] The men worked a normal five-day week with a 'bonus day' on a Saturday. Work normally began at 7am, but long before the arrival of his workforce, Bram had been round the pit clearing up falls and getting the men's work places ready.[17] During the day he performed the work of winder, unloader, blacksmith and office clerk and was the one who received all visitors. When the men had completed their shifts, between 2pm and 3pm, he was back down the pit 'tidying up' and checking the timbering. When the surface coal stocking area had been filled to capacity, the National Coal Board was notified and transport was arranged for its removal to its designated customers.

Peggy Tub Main received much publicity in both the local and national press. A proud man, Bram was always willing to discuss his mining operation with anyone. His endeavours were even the subject of a Home Service radio programme in November 1947.[18] The media cover led to interest abroad, his fame reaching the USA, Mexico and continental Europe. Four newsreel companies showed Peggy Tub Main in their local cinema news reviews (Figure 5).

Figure 5. Bram Pashley working in the 43″ thick Top Beamshaw seam by candlelight, 1948.

Coal production increased at the little pit and in 1949 output passed the sixty tons a week mark.[19] The fear of penetrating areas of old workings was always a major worry for mine management, especially at collieries where the seams were at shallow depth and had little previous documentation. In January 1950 a new heading, which was being driven westwards from the base of shaft No 2, broke into such an area.[20] These were workings from Thomas Firth's Durkar Colliery which had worked the Top Beamshaw seam in the area towards the end of the previous century and about which there was minimal information available. Slowly at first, but with gathering impetus, the water which had accumulated over many years was

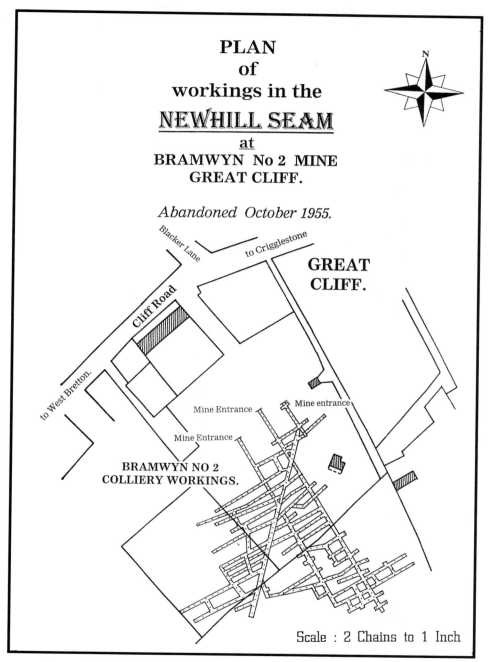

Figure 6. Bramwyn No 2 mine, Great Cliff. Abandoned in October 1955.

soon to inundate the underground galleries of Bram's colliery. A rapid exodus from the mine following the increasing rise in floodwater had curtailed any chance of salvaging valuable equipment.[21] Eventually the floodwaters stabilised and pumping commenced in an attempt to reduce the level. At first it appeared that the problem might be alleviated, the level dropping considerably during pumping operations. However after a while the pumps became overwhelmed and the level began rising again. It soon became apparent that clearing the flood water was an insuperable task. After much deliberation it was decided that there was no alternative other than to curtail pumping and abandon the mine.[22] Peggy Tub Main had been in operation for barely three years, during which time it had produced in the order of 4,500 tons of coal.

It was not, however, to be the end of Bram's mining endeavours. At the other end of the parish at Great Cliff, Arthur Wilcock, a former overman at Crigglestone Colliery, had exposed a seam of coal while excavating a trench through his allotment.[24] The seam proved to be the Newhill or Steam Coal, having a total thickness including dirt bands of over eight feet. The seam was not as good a quality as the Top Beamshaw seam mined at Peggy Tub Main, but at that time it had a ready and available market. Arthur, a close friend of Bram, soon had willing ears in support for his proposal to sink three surface drifts to work the coal. An agreement between the two was drawn up and signed in February 1951.[25] The colliery was to be known as Bramwyn No. 2 (Figure 6). In late February 1951 the mine was given the sanction of the National Coal Board, and with a workforce of six miners commenced production (Figure 7).[26]

Bram's ingenuity was soon in evidence at Bramwyn No. 2 where he designed and installed a haulage engine – the ever-popular Austin Seven unit converted and made capable of drawing four fully-loaded tubs from the workings up the incline to the drift entrance.[27] For a time Bram settled into the new project with his usual enthusiasm and fervour, but his heart was never far from his original venture and Peggy Tub Main still stood as an everyday reminder of his earlier aspirations. His decision to make a further attempt to de-water the workings there is not too difficult to comprehend.

On 5 April 1952 the partnership at Great Cliff was dissolved,[28] though the colliery worked on with partners Arthur Wilcock and Ambrose Gill of Boat House Farm, Durkar, until its eventual abandonment in January 1954.[29]

In the meantime, Bram, anxious to revive his original venture at Calder Grove and with a view to raising capital in the interim,

Figure 7. Bramwyn No 2 mine, Great Cliff, looking towards No 1 drift entrance, 1951.

purchased a coach.[30] This was hired to local organisations, usually for seaside excursions, though a ready use was made of it for transporting millworkers and schoolchildren. During the Festival of Britain in 1951, Bram organised a weekly trip from the Merry Citie to London.

By August 1954 Bram was successfully lowering the floodwater at Peggy Tub Main.[31] Attacked by a varied array of pumping equipment, including a pump fashioned from the steering column of a taxi and motor-cycle gearbox, the floodwater was made to recede.

The lack of ventilation over the four years since the inundation, had resulted in the accumulation of pockets of mine gas in isolated areas of the workings. To clear these concentrations, Bram devised a ventilation system which comprised primarily an old washing boiler and a quarter horse-power electric motor. His system proved to be highly successful.[32] Salvage and reconstruction work slowly progressed. A visit from a *Yorkshire Evening Post* reporter in August 1954 found Bram confident that his mine would soon be in full operation again and looking forward to the National Coal Board reinstating his licence which he had relinquished on the abandonment of the mine in 1951.[33]

To assist with any future removal of floodwater from the mine, Bram excavated a fifteen-foot deep sump at the base of the shaft to act as a collecting place for any subsequent inundations. A pump was placed permanently at the base of the sump ready for immediate use. Just when the situation at Peggy Tub Main seemed to be reaching a satisfactory outcome, the inconceivable was to happen. A week of heavy and persistent rain – heavy enough to cause extensive flooding in parts of the parish – had caused a build up of pressure in the old mineworkings of Thomas Firth. The brick stopping which had been installed to repair the previous breach in the old workings failed and floodwater again inundated the mine, this time filling the sump, flooding the workings and backing up the shaft to within twelve feet of the surface. Realising the serious nature of the situation and its implications, Bram was left with little option but to abandon his mine again, a decision he made with great disappointment in February 1955.[34]

Though in 1956 Bram was to make a successful application for a licence to work coal at Woodmoor, Newmillerdam,[35] taking on and defeating the mighty County Planning Department in the process, his venture at Woodmoor Hill drift mine was to be short lived.[36]

Figure 8. Newmillerdam, Bushcliff Wood, remnants of former mining activities. January 1998. *Keith Wainwright.*

(Figure 8) It is perhaps fitting that Bram's final days in mining were to be spent in close proximity to where his childhood dreams had been nurtured.

Bramwell Arthur Pashley, miner, inventor and instigator extraordinary, died at Newmillerdam in October 1981. Of his former collieries, Bramwell Nos. 1 and 2 now lie under the earthworks of the M1 motorway. The site of Woodmoor Hill drift mine, his final mining venture, is now barely discernible, nature having over the years reclaimed her own.

Notes and References

1. Mine Records Office, Bretby, and 1849 OS.
2. Chapelthorpe St.James Church Registers.
3. Mine Records Office, Bretby, plan no. 8775.
4. *Wakefield Express* 19.2.1955
5. Pashley Brothers' account books, in private hands.
6. *Daily Mail*, 6.10.1047.
7. *Ibid.*
8. Weekly News, 11.10.1947
9. Mine Records Office, Bretby, and *Wakefield Express* 6.10.1947.
10. *Wakefield Express* 4.10.1947
11. *Yorkshire Evening Post*, 10.8.1947.
12. *Yorkshire Evening Post*, 6.10.1947.
13. *Yorkshire Evening Post*, 5.6.1950.
14. *Wakefield Express*, 12.6.1948.
15. *Ibid.*
16. Coal Industry Nationalisation Act.
17. *Wakefield Express*, 12.6.1948.
18. *Radio Times*, 14.11.1947.
19. *Yorkshire Evening Post*, 5.8.1954.
20. Mine Records Office, Bretby, plan no. NE 64.
21. *Yorkshire Evening Post*, 5.6.1950.
22. *Wakefield Express*, 3.6.1950.
23. *Ibid.*
24. *Telegraph and Argus*, 22.5.1951.
25. Partnership agreement, February 1951, in private hands.
26. *Telegraph and Argus*, 22.2.1951
27. *Ibid.*
28. Agreement dated 5.4.1952, in private hands.
29. Mine Records Office, Bretby, plan no NE 188.
30. *Yorkshire Observer*, 5.5.1951.
31. *Yorkshire Evening Post*, 5.8.1954.
32. *Ibid.*
33. Mine Records Office, Bretby, plan no. NE 64.
34. *Yorkshire Evening Post*, 16.2.1955.
35. *Yorkshire Observer*, 27.3.1956.
36. Mine Records Office, Bretby, plan no. NE 515.

5. WAKEFIELD'S GARDEN CITY SCHEMES

by Kate Taylor

THE CONCEPT OF THE GARDEN CITY was popular in the early years of the twentieth century. It embodied the then-novel idea of attractive detached or semi-detached houses, each with its own cottage garden, in pleasant suburbs at low cost for ordinary working people.[1]

Garden cities epitomised a contemporary ideal of the good life. It was thought that they offered a healthful contrast to the typical terraced streets and paved yards of the town. They were seen as agents for social reform and they were pioneered by men like the Quaker George Cadbury, the cocoa and chocolate manufacturer who created a garden city at Bourneville in the 1890s.

This, and other garden-city developments, formed the focus of a discussion at a meeting of Wakefield Paxton Society in January 1908.[2] But it was a number of local Quakers associated with Wakefield's New Scarborough Adult School, which had been founded in 1905, who were the prime movers behind the first of the two Wakefield garden city schemes.[3] The Adult School was a branch of a national movement, described in 1907 by Tom Bryan of Bourneville as religious, political and social, but not a church, sect or denomination.

Early in 1908 promoters of this first Wakefield garden city scheme approached Wakefield Corporation with a proposal to buy a disused sewage farm at New Scarborough, but this was rejected.[4] The sale by Messrs Bradley and Craven in May 1808 of a large plot of undeveloped land, bounded by Flanshaw Lane and Dewsbury Road, provided the opportunity they needed. (Figure 1) The site, acquired initially by Herbert Elliott of New Park Farm, Welbeck, was transferred to Mrs Ruth Morritt, another Quaker, whose husband George was a builder with substantial property interests in the Halton, Whitkirk and Temple Newsam areas of Leeds, and who attended the Great Wilson Street Quaker meeting in Leeds.[5]

Three avenues were planned, each as cul de sacs with access to Dewsbury Road. These were named Wilhelm, Oakleigh and Ashleigh. Individual building plots, of 600 to 1,000 square yards, were designated along these avenues and on Flanshaw Lane itself. Land was to be sold at a shilling per square yard. The price, it was

MESSᴿˢ BRADLEY & CRAVEN Lᵀᴰ

WAKEFIELD.

SALE PLAN of LOTS 34 to 44 INCLUSIVE

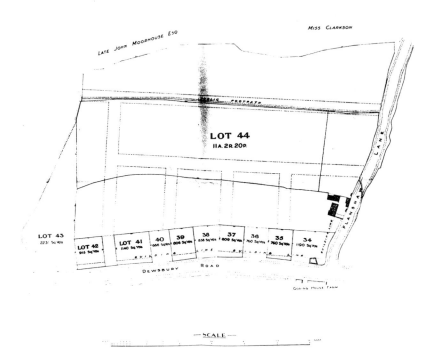

Figure 1. This page, from the catalogue for the sale of some of Bradley and Craven's land-holding in 1908, shows the lots which became Wakefield's first garden city. *The John Goodchild Collection.*

reported, would include the making-up of the road surfaces, drainage and the provision of kerbs and grass verges. Advances from speculative builders were to be refused. Those who bought plots were, however, free to employ the builder of their choice.[6] The only restrictions seem to have been that they should adhere to an agreed building line and should border their land with privet hedging (Figure 2).

Albert E Halliday, a carrier then living in Henry Street and a key

Figure 2. Privet hedges remain a feature of Poplar Avenue, 1998. *Kate Taylor.*

member of the Wakefield garden-city pioneers, organised a trip to Bourneville in August 1908 for 400 local people.[7]

The initial take-up of plots, all in Wilhelm Avenue, must have seemed encouraging. Three of the trustees of the New Scarborough Adult School were quick to acquire sites: they were Halliday himself, William Harris Blackburn (a reporter), and John Atkinson (an upholsterer and carpet fitter). Two more residents from Henry Street bought plots: James Ayers (a painter) and Samuel Berridge (a postman). Other early purchases were made by Edmund Allsop of Manygates Terrace (mechanic), Harry Bastow of Whitehall Street (a joiner), Thomas Bastow (a moulder), William Blockley of Dewsbury Road (an insurance agent), Samuel Coates of Lincoln Street (a wire worker), Henry Just of Cambridge Street (an asylum attendant) and Joseph Marsh (a farmer) of Balne Lane. Halliday's wife contracted to buy a plot adjoining his and the couple built a pair of semi-detached houses.[8]

Larger plots were halved to bring sites within reach of the poorest of the participants. Sums paid for land ranged from a modest £20 for 400 square yards, paid by Harry Bastow, to £47 10s for an 850 square yard plot purchased by Samuel Coates.

But further interest in the scheme was slow to develop. There was no public transport to the area which was separated from Wakefield in those days by green fields. As yet there were no shops in the immediate vicinity and although a bowling green was mooted, public houses were specifically excluded from the area. By 1913 when the Morritts established the Garden City Estate Company (Wakefield), only Wilhelm Avenue and the north side of Oakleigh Avenue had been developed and none of the corner sites adjoining Dewsbury Road itself had been taken.[9]

Nonetheless it was in 1913 that a second garden city scheme was begun. This was the work of the then Mayor of Wakefield, Edwin Lodge Hirst, who was a corn merchant, and the Bishop of Wakefield, George Rodney Eden. The pair took a further substantial area of undeveloped land which lay to the north of the original garden city, again bordering Dewsbury Road and including what are now Hirst Road and Eden Avenue (Figures 3 and 4). This was to be the Wakefield Garden Suburb and, as at the first garden city, was designed to enable artisans to buy plots of land cheaply and to build pleasant houses where they could create attractive gardens. The first

Figure 3. Hirst Road, named after Edwin Lodge Hirst, Mayor of Wakefield in 1913, 1996. *Kate Taylor.*

Figure 4. Eden Avenue, named after George Rodney Eden, Bishop of Wakefield from 1897 to 1928, 1996. *Kate Taylor.*

of these plots was taken by T W Gant, a corporation labourer.[10]

Development came to a standstill during the Great War. The only significant change was in the name of Wilhelm Avenue which, abandoning the name of the German Kaiser, became the more acceptable Poplar Avenue which it remains today.

After the war plots, whether in the Bishop's scheme or the adjacent scheme of the Quakers, sold only slowly. It was not until 1930 that the then Diocesan Registrar, W H Coles, who had become a trustee of the Garden Suburb, was able to repay the loans which had financed the Eden-Hirst venture and complete the road making.[11]

In 1925 a leading Wakefield builder, George Crook, acquired several plots on Flanshaw Lane from the Garden City Company, erecting a detached bungalow and a pair of very handsome semis adjoining the ginnel which runs from Flanshaw Lane to Eden Avenue.[12] The firm of George Crook had been founded in the 1870s as joiners and builders. One of George Crook's earliest investments was in Lincoln Street where he built a terrace of nine houses and a shop, selling them a year later. Between 1901 and 1903 Crook built the terraces in Whitehall Street, Dewsbury Road. In 1907 he bought the Westgate Brick Company which had opened a brick quarry in Dewsbury Road three years earlier. As a contractor he built many public buildings in Wakefield, including the Police Headquarters in Wood Street and the Empire Theatre in Kirkgate, later to become the Gaumont Cinema. The firm was also the chief contractor for the Lupset, Peacock and Portobello council-house estates. In 1928 the firm became George Crook and Sons, with Hargreaves, the younger George, and Colin becoming partners. George Crook died in 1930.[13]

In 1932 the Crooks bought almost every remaining plot from the Garden City Company, including the wholly-undeveloped Ashleigh Avenue, the one remaining plot at the east end of Oakleigh Avenue, and the plots at the Dewsbury Road end of Oakleigh and Poplar Avenues.[14] Here, using bricks from their own quarry, they built a series of attractive, but identical, semi-detached houses to let. Thus it is that the Garden City includes a range of very individual houses of the 1910s and 1920s and also a fleet of identical 1930s semis (Figure 5).

At the same time, John Archer, a cocoa matting manufacturer, who had recently built Flanshaw Lodge, bought up all the garden city land on Flanshaw Lane between his own property and the ginnel, thus giving him control of any development near his own house. The plots were bought a year later by George Taylor (the present writer's father, who was an electrical engineer working for the National Grid)

Figure 5. Identical semi-detached houses in Ashleigh Avenue built by George Crook and Sons in the 1930s, 1998. *Kate Taylor.*

and Horace Wright, an auctioneer.

In 1933 the Crook firm bought sixteen acres of land from James Walter Watson of Flanshaw House, laying out Pinewood, Beechwood and Oakwood Avenues, not quite a garden city but nonetheless another very pleasant suburban development.[15]

Notes and References

1. M Miller, *Letchworth: the first garden city* (1989).
2. *Wakefield and West Riding Herald*, 4 January 1908.
3. Papers of the New Scarborough Adult School, Brotherton Library, Leeds University.
4. *Wakefield and West Riding Herald*, 27 June 1908.
5. Letter of 11 December 1992 to the author from the library of the Religious Society of Friends. West Riding Registry of Deeds, 1908 Vol. 30 p70.
6. *Wakefield and West Riding Herald,* 12 September 1908.
7. *Wakefield Express,* 22 August 1908.
8. West Riding Registry of Deeds. 1908 Vol. 35, p324.
9. West Riding Registry of Deeds. 1914 Vol 4, p538.
10. West Riding Registry of Deeds. 1913 Vol. 54, p1018.
11. Letter of 20 December 1931 from W H Coles.
12. West Riding Registry of Deeds. 1925 Vol. 21, p569.
13. K Taylor (ed.) *Wakefield District Heritage*, (1979) Vol.II, p44-45.
14. West Riding Registry of Deeds 1932 Vol. 116, p258 and p261.
15. West Riding Registry of Deeds 1933 Vol. 49, p737

6. THE POPLAR AVENUE ACC CLUB

by Pearl Putscher

THE OLSON FAMILY ARRIVED in Wakefield from Halifax in August 1939, a month before war broke out. My parents, my brother John, then eleven, and myself (thirteen) moved into 5 Poplar Avenue, Dewsbury Road, part of the 'garden city' in the area known as Flanshaw. My mother quickly discovered the house had been built in 1907 by a Quaker family. This was to pacify me as I deeply resented having to leave Stannary Hall where I was born and which was 300 years old. I loved old things. We children had to make friends and quickly did so by attending St George's Church, Lupset, and Thornes House School. But our main centre of activity was the peaceful, tree-lined Poplar Avenue. Here it was that the Club was born:

Anchor and Crown Club
25/8/40
> *Dear Pearl,*
> *Do you think it possible to attend a meeting of the Anchor and Crown Club today at 3pm.*
> > *From*
> > *Anchor and Crown Club.*

> *P.S. Will you please tell your brother.*

The letter was sent by Margaret Irving (twelve) and Bettina Gibson (twelve) who lived next door to one another at the bottom of the Avenue. When I questioned them about the title of the Club, they told me that the exercise book they would write the minutes in had ACC on the front and they could only come up with Anchor and Crown Club. To me it sounded like a pub sign. Alright, our parents did frequent the Palm Court of the *Strafford Arms* in the Bull Ring, but with its green plants and comfortable sofas, presided over by the indomitable Miss Jackson, that was an entirely different ambience. I was studying Latin for my School Certificate and after some thought came up with Amicae at Comites Claritas, which I thought translated as Friends and Companions of Brightness, and it remained such. It was very bad Latin.

The first meetings were held on the Gibsons' back lawn , and at some stage, probably when the weather got cooler, we were able to persuade my mother to let us have our spare room. We gained more members – Kathleen Spencer (twelve) who lived down the ginnel in 'Crook's' estate[1], Winifred Rothwell from Lupset (fourteen) and Clarence Le Clerque, an exotic figure who had been evacuated from the Channel Islands to live with the schoolmaster who lived next door to us and his wife, Mr and Mrs Hall. Clarence was a worldly wise fifteen and smoked, which necessitated my putting up a notice in the Clubroom, 'No smoking'. As I recall we never spoke to him about Jersey and we never discussed the war.

The ACC Club, I note, looking back at the minutes written in longhand in the green-backed exercise book, was highly organised:

> *All members agreed that in this present time, when 'the rule of the people' was so important, the Club should uphold the nation's cause of Democracy; therefore it was decided that no leader should be elected, that all members however old or young, the first member as last member, should vote alike and be recognised as equals, and that a president should be elected once a month, to keep order and receive suggestions. This record, like the American Declaration of Independence and the French Rights of Man, marks the beginning of a new epoch of the ACC, an epoch of Democracy and Independence.*
>
> *The next business on hand was to 'reshuffle the Cabinet', as it were, and propose candidates for the various offices. All votes were unanimous. Winifred, who, we are happy to announce, will be a regular comer in the future, is in charge of the Dramatic Society. We hope to make great progress in this sphere and hope to produce a play in time. Margaret, who will be capable of handling them, is in charge of the Expiditions (sic), of which we hope to (have) many enjoyable ones in the coming season. Kathleen will be librarian.*
>
> *Betty is given the games to organise. We hope she will have plenty of scope both in our outings and in the Clubroom. Clarence, who, in view of his living with a Warden should de very well, was voted ARP manager. It is hoped that, although we may never have cause to use them, we might organise a Fire Squad and a First Aid Party. John was elected treasurer and we sincerely hope that he will have a busy time. Pearl, as secretary, is in her element and expects to have many thrilling episodes to record.*
>
> *After this Margaret disclosed that a mysterious parcel, which had been the cause of many curious glances, contained bottles of lemonade.*

At once glasses were filled and a toast, The Club, was proposed.
So with much joviality the Club departed.

Code of Rules

These rules may be enlarged, extended, but not altered at any time by the President.
i)   All members shall be regarded as equals, politically and socially.
ii) Every member must think and work for the improvement of the Club.
Persons not actively engaged in support of it cannot be regarded as members.
iii) All members shall have the privilege of free thought as individuals, but as a Club they must abide by the wishes of the majority.
iv) At meetings or outings it is understood that members keep together except when agreed by the whole Club.
v)   Secrets and cryptical allusions are not desired at meetings or outings. They breed slyness and foolishness and leave discomfort and embarrassment.

The rules were strict and those who could be accused of poor attendance or being quarrelsome were 'helped' to resign. Some hopeful boys never got in!

Long term members included Malcolm Urquhart, my nine-year old cousin from South Shields, sent down to my mother by her sister Daisy when the bombing got too bad on the Tyne, and Derek Schofield (twelve) who had been in hospital at the same time as Margaret when both had Scarlet Fever, and who lived at the bottom of Broadway, Lupset. He was soon seen as an Ideas Man and a Useful Member.

We had occasional visitors, like my schoolfriend from Halifax, Kathleen Clay (thirteen) and John 'Willie' Williams, John's friend from Thornes Church Scouts. Some came and went. Clarence was an erratic member who made up wild excuses for not attending and was drummed out. Winifred, our musical member, who played the piano so beautifully and helped to write a song with us, quarreled with Clarence and left, but returned when he went. These two were older than the rest, who were mostly uncomplicated.

The Club was a focus for the lives of myself, my brother and the other members and our understanding parents must have been grateful that this tightly-knit group kept us out of mischief and our minds off the war.

Our pocket money was something like a shilling a week and we paid threepence a week in subscriptions. So far as the war was concerned, we largely ignored it at first. Air raid warnings caused a frisson of excitement at night, when John and I and Vick the dog would dive into the cupboard under the stairs to sleep. Once when we were meeting in daylight in Betti's garden we heard the drone of aircraft and the thump of bombs and decided 'they' were bombing Dewsbury cutting up the road, and all fled in opposite directions to the safety of our homes. At school air-raid shelters had been dug in the playing fields and ARP practices, when we would all file down into the ground, gas mask boxes over our shoulders, were solemn but exciting occasions. (Speaking of gas masks, I often had to use their safety pins to fix my suspenders if they broke on my twenty-minute walk to school!) We listened to the news on the radio, and in particular to Children's Hour, from 5pm to 6pm, when there were frequent appeals for money for the War Effort. One of Wakefield's money-raising efforts was a German bomb erected in the Bull Ring for passers-by to insert their loose change into a slot. We were particularly interested in this as we believed it to be the very bomb which had dropped in Kathleen Hogg's garden in Chantry Road, Lupset estate in December 1940. There had been no damage and nobody hurt and at lunchtime the next day we deviated from our usual route home to go and peer at the crater. Some of the boys jumped in. Only later did we discover that it was an unexploded bomb!

Security of information was very important and therefore a local tragedy never reached our ears. This was that two bombs fell on 14 March 1941, demolished nine houses in Thornes Road, killed six people and injured fifteen.[2] This incident was less than a mile from our house and on the edge of our school park, and yet we knew nothing. It was 1991 before I knew these details from an article in the *Wakefield Express*.

Looking through the battered green file that we kept our records in I came across the Minute Book, the Expedition Book, and the Who's Who. I have a carefully preserved roll of bus tickets commemorating the time we got on a bus, asked 'Where does a penny end?' and got to a strange place called Calder Grove where we enjoyed a ramble by a stream and 'sunbathed on a grass-covered slag heap'. Another bunch of tickets were for seven pence. Where did we go on that occasion? Was it to Coxley Valley where we dammed up a little stream and concocted a game called 'the other side of Jordan'? I believe we had to jump across without getting our feet wet, apropos the Children of Israel. Many of our games had Biblical themes, probably because we attended confirmation classes (and some members were Roman Catholics). Thus there is reference to 'Matthew, Mark, Luke and John', 'Proverbs', and 'Jacob and Rachel' which almost developed into a vulgar brawl, though none of us remembers now how we played these. Those games we do remember are 'Murder' and 'Sardines'.

When the Club was held in our own homes, space was limited, hence the search for new premises. On 24 May 1941, during a meeting held in the Olsons' garage, Flanshaw Hall was mentioned:(Figure 1)

> *They trekked over to view it..and even got as far as knocking at the front door but their nerve failed and they ran!*

In June the old house in 'Mr.Olson's works' was suggested. This was at George Lee and Sons at the bottom of Westgate where my father was Chief Engineer. Needless to say we could not have that as it involved going through the mill, but we tried! It was not until September that a real possibility arose:

> *Derek had negotiated with the Parochial Council of St.George's Church, Lupset, and they had generously consented to let us have the Choir Vestry! Ah Happy Day! Farewell to the draughty haunts of late.*

The church premises suited us very well, especially as Mr Whitworth occasionally allowed us to go into the big hall in the Crypt, which was

Figure 1. Flanshaw Old Hall, demolished in 1949   *Courtesy of Mrs Joyce Taylor.*

Figure 2. St George's Church, Lupset, consecrated 26 September 1936. The church was designed by Sir Charles Nicholson and built by George Crook and Sons. 1998. *Kate Taylor*

perfect for our games of Sardines and Murder when the blackout was in place. In due course we also explored the Boiler Room, the Coffin Room and various corners. The big room was ideal for rehearsing the play and other concert items and we always left the place as we found it, the furniture in its rightful place and the blackout wrestled with, like the well brought up children we were! I have a receipt for two shillings and sixpence from the Lupset PCC with a note from Mr Bramham, the Treasurer, thanking us for our donation to church expenses (Figure 2).Thumbing through the green file of Memorabilia I find a price list: Bath Crystals 1s 9d, Tray Cover 1s 6d, Pin Cushion 3d, Tea Cosy 2s 3d, Pokerwork Pictures 2s, Kettle Holders 8d, Bookends 1s. Ah! This was the Sale of Goods held in Poplar Avenue on 26 April 1941 for the War Effort. The goods were all hand made at our meetings, the boys doing woodwork and painting and the girls knitting or doing embroidery or pokerwork. My father donated a dozen precious eggs to raffle and we raised £2. A second sale later that summer benefited from the sale of jars of my mother's raspberry jam, made with fruit from our garden and molasses donated by the Garthwaites at No 1. Mr. Garthwaite was a brewer at Clark's Brewery and the molasses was extraneous to his production, he said.

The most enjoyable money-raising effort was the Concert, incorporating the play. This, *The Man in the Bowler Hat,* by A A

Milne, was in production from 5 July until its appearance in Olsons'
garage on 6 December 1941. Of course we had other things to do
during the summer months and not all characters turned up to
rehearsals, but all in all we stuck at it and I was pleased with my
production. John had bright ideas for lighting. Betti and Margaret
could supply the costume, and my Dad agreed to the use of our
garage:

*A book of play acting was consulted and found to be helpful in regard to
make-up, dress, properties and acting.*

6 December 1941
The Massive Concert
Entertainment
For the Ministry of Aircraft Production

Prologue	*Members of the ACC Club*
Monologue	*Derek, The Green Eye of the Little Yellow God*
Recorder Duet	*Winifred and Margaret, The Grasmere Carol*
Sketch	*Members of the ACC, Humbugs*
Monologue	*John, the Glory of the Garden*
Diversion	*The Fate of the Criminal (shadow play)*
Recorder Solo	*Margaret, Scots Wha' hae*
Play	*The Man in the Bowler Hat*

John: John O.		*Mary: Betti*	
Hero: Margaret		*Heroine: Kathleen*	
Bad Man: Derek		*Chief Villain: Pearl*	
Man in the			
Bowler Hat: John P.			
Epilogue		*Members of the ACC*	

We ended with a spirited rendering of Ravel's Bolero, all of us
contributing, with two recorders and an assortment of tin trays, and
my young cousin Malcolm on a noisy drum. We charged threepence
for our neighbours to sit on chairs placed half in and half out of the
garage door, and raised about thirty shillings.

Another money-raising effort we heard about was collecting herbs
to be sold to chemists:

*We cheerfully started to dig up those most provoking weeds,
dandelions. Thanks to the perseverance of all members, one lb was
collected.*

There is no mention of how much was raised by this effort! What is clear, however, is that we did raise money and it went to the right place, ie the War Effort. Here in the green file is an envelope postmarked 24 Dec 1942, its war economy label addressed to me, and enclosing a receipt for £2 15s in respect of a Gift for Aircraft, sent from the Ministry of Aircraft Production (Figures 3 and 4). BBC Radio Children's Hour broadcast acknowledgments of donations sent in by children. We listened avidly to hear our Club's contribution mentioned, and it was.

Another yellowing scrap of paper falls from the green file. The cricket match! The paper is a cutting from the *Wakefield Express* referring to a charity cricket match at College Grove on 20 September 1941. The Club attended in force (Betti's father being on the committee). Several county men were playing, including Smailes, Butters, Barber and Leyland. An autographed bat was to be raffled and by clubbing up our Club subscriptions, a ticket no 146 was purchased. It won! But the ticket was lost. There ensued a prolonged search of the field but it was never found. It must have been our shining honest faces and powers of rhetoric which persuaded the organisers to agree to our claim to the bat. The bat is still in my possession, as Club secretary. (Figure 5) It carries the names of twenty-three cricketers and an inscription, 'Presented to the ACC Club at College Grove, Wakefield, September 20th 1941', all duly varnished. The raffle raised £13 for war charities.

A riffle through the pink-backed Expedition Book helps me to relive many

Figure 3. Letter of 24 December 1942 from the Ministry of Aircraft Production, to the author recording that donations by the ACC Club had reached £6 6s. *From the ACC archive.*

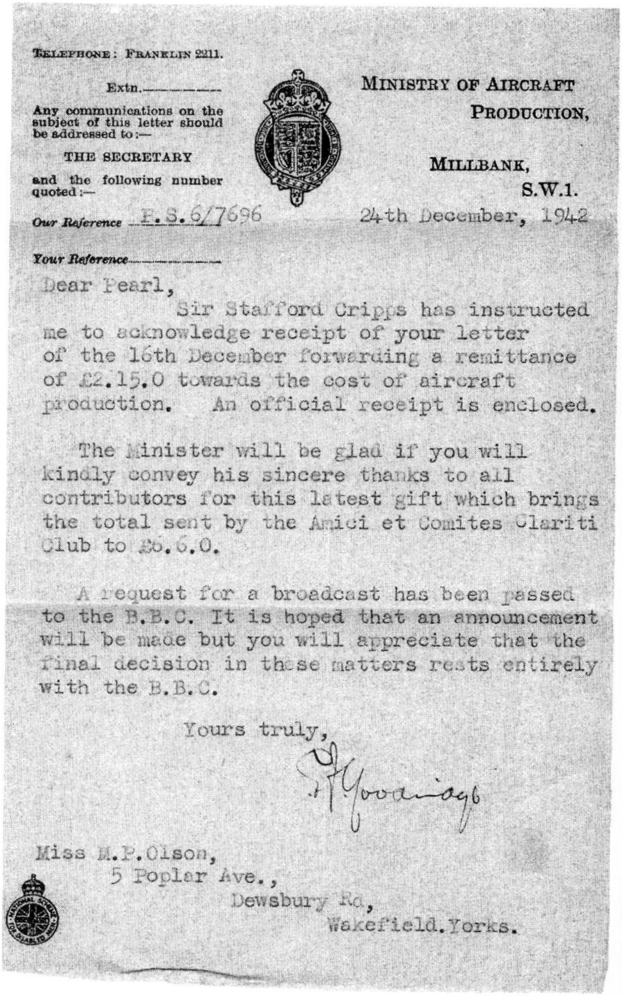

TELEPHONE: FRANKLIN 2211.

Extn.

Any communications on the subject of this letter should be addressed to:—

THE SECRETARY

and the following number quoted:—

MINISTRY OF AIRCRAFT PRODUCTION,

MILLBANK, S.W.1.

Our Reference F.S.6/7696

24th December, 1942

Your Reference

Dear Pearl,

Sir Stafford Cripps has instructed me to acknowledge receipt of your letter of the 16th December forwarding a remittance of £2.15.0 towards the cost of aircraft production. An official receipt is enclosed.

The Minister will be glad if you will kindly convey his sincere thanks to all contributors for this latest gift which brings the total sent by the Amici et Comites Clariti Club to £6.6.0.

A request for a broadcast has been passed to the B.B.C. It is hoped that an announcement will be made but you will appreciate that the final decision in these matters rests entirely with the B.B.C.

Yours truly,

Miss M.P.Olson,
5 Poplar Ave.,
Dewsbury Rd,
Wakefield.Yorks.

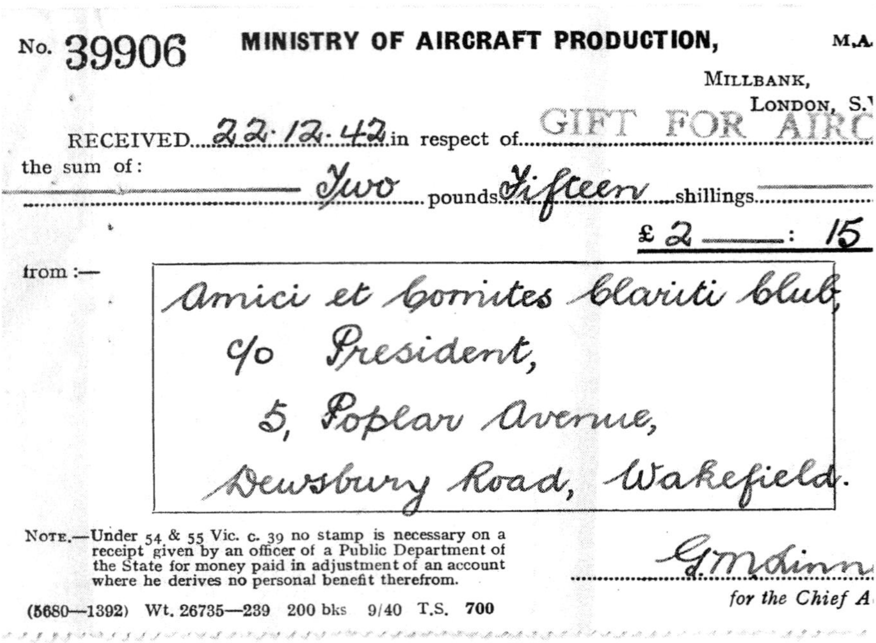

No. **39906**   **MINISTRY OF AIRCRAFT PRODUCTION,**   M.A.

MILLBANK,

LONDON, S.

RECEIVED *22.12.42* in respect of *GIFT FOR AIRC*

the sum of:

Two pounds *Fifteen* shillings

£ *2* — : *15*

from :—

Amici et Comites Clariti Club,
c/o President,
5, Poplar Avenue,
Dewsbury Road, Wakefield.

NOTE.—Under 54 & 55 Vic. c. 39 no stamp is necessary on a
receipt given by an officer of a Public Department of
the State for money paid in adjustment of an account
where he derives no personal benefit therefrom.

(5680—1392) Wt. 26735—239 200 bks 9/40 T.S. **700**

G. M. Ainn

for the Chief A

Figure 4. Receipt from the Ministry of Aircraft Production for £2 15s
donated as a 'gift for aircraft' by the Amici at Comites Clariti.
From the ACC archive.

memories of our outdoor antics. In spring we used to meander down
Flanshaw Lane and across large fields to end up at the top of
Dewsbury Road and so home. Invariably we would end up being
shouted at by some strange fellow who threatened to 'have us up in
Wood Street'. None of this made any sense to us until the day I
decided to stand my ground and cope with the fellow in plus-fours.
I discovered we had been trespassing on Low Laithes golf course:

and by dint of extending my sympathies, managed to cool him.

After all, I explained, there had been no notices warning 'Trespassers
will be prosecuted'. Another famous day was 25 May 1941:

Margaret, Betti, Kathleen, Malcolm, John and Pearl set out for
Spring Woods. They took the bus so far along Flanshaw Lane and
walked the rest, picking rhubarb as they went. It rained as they
reached the woods, but when it cleared they partook of rhubarb,
biscuits, lemonade and liquorice water. After climbing trees and
playing tracking, Kathleen endeavoured to pick some bluebells but

Figure 5. The autographed bat, inscribed 'Presented to the ACC Club at College Grove, Wakefield, September 20th 1941, 1998. *Kate Taylor.*

John and she differed as to whether the white parts of the stem should be taken and a fierce quarrel resulted. Alack! A long walk home.

We were all for a bit of excitement and in July 1941 we decided to have a midnight feast in the Avenue unbeknown to our parents. I made the slushy sandwiches and John bottled the lemonade. We hid it behind the settee in the drawing room where casement windows were easy to open onto the garden. John and Malcolm were to keep each other awake with a wet flannel and I had a string attached to my big toe and tied to the bed. The Expedition Book contains Margaret's record:

8 July 1941. Tonight is the night which stands out most in the memory of the members (at least Betti's and mine). Nobody knew of our expeditions that night as Betti and I crept out of bed at 2.30am. Father was snoring loudly, Mother ready to wake at the slightest noise. Cases in hand we crept downstairs and proceeded to dress quickly in the kitchen. I, by the way, had picked up Mother's shoes in the haste and had to wear them.

Now came the job of unbolting and unlocking the back door. This was done successfully and we crept down the drive.

The night was very still; a grey mist hung round the houses which looked so darkly sinister against it.

We reached the meeting place without mishap and proceeded to call the Olsons by a series of short hisses. Nobody arrived!!!

After waiting 20 minutes we returned home and undressed, got our cases safely under the bed and into it ourselves. There was nobody to wake you with a wet flannel and say it was your turn to go on shift so peace was restored once more.

Later it was found that P and J (Pearl and John) couldn't come 'cos Mr. and Mrs. Olson didn't go to bed until 4am having been to a dinner dance with Bettina's parents, Mr. and Mrs. Gibson.

A year or two later Betti's father came across this entry and tackled my parents about these 'disgusting goings on'. And it was all so innocent!

It should be mentioned here that our picnics were famous for our own 'slushy sandwiches', consisting of lettuce, tomato and cucumber, home grown, saturated with lots of salad cream. Meat, cheese and eggs were on ration, you see. And, of course, a bottle of liquorice water made from sticks of liquorice root from Pontefract soaked in water.

We were hardy creatures and winter weather held no fears for us. Thus:

13 December 1941. This evening Margaret kept us guessing. She had hinted all day about a friend of hers whom she and her mother had met the previous evening and whose nickname was Wol. Tonight she gathered us together, Winifred, Betti, Kathleen, Derek and Pearl, and led us in the twilight, indeed, darkness, up unfamiliar ways. At the corner of an unknown lane, she halted us, left us and disappeared into the gloom. Our consternation was evident from the way we spoke in whispers, clung to each other shivering, and feared for Margaret's safety. Whilst speculating as to who this mysterious personage might be, there came to us the shrill hoot of an owl. Kathleen informed us that there was an owl in the wood nearby and Derek identified the shriek of the male. At this time Winnie speculated as to whether Margaret was hooting as she did it remarkably well. At once Derek realised that Wol could be twisted to Owl and we at last recognised our new friend. Soon Margaret returned and, on being congratulated, led us to the wood, where she called the owl and he answered. This remarkable piece of nature study thrilled us all.

In January there was an account of a bike trip to Sandal Castle where 'a staggish' game of hide and seek was enjoyed. In February Derek instigated tracking as a diversion. Two would set off and at twenty minute intervals other couples would start, following signs left by the hares.

15 February 1942. As today was a holiday, Margaret, Derek, John and Pearl decided to go tracking. Margaret and Derek set off and Pearl and John followed in twenty minutes. Up Eden Avenue, up

Dewsbury Road. At the Colliery, M and D were espied, who angrily told P and J to go back. In 5 mins time, P and J again followed. A letter was found. 'Bus to Shepherd's Hill.' No bus conductress seemed to know the place and P and J set off to walk down Queen's Drive. 4 people were asked, including a 'zombie' and at last they trekked across fields and fields, back to Dewsbury Rd. Here no trace could be found of signs until, by chance, a pink arrow was found along a cart track. Merrily they rolled along, until the arrows stopped outside a red house. Giving up the quest, P and J saw a farmer shovelling turnips, followed a frozen stream, followed a path, heard no sound, rested on a track, sketched a house and ended up in a mysterious village. A post woman said it was Gawthorpe and the travellers found themselves on Dewsbury Road. A fourpence-halfpenny bus ride took them home, where they found M and D were home and they had scoured the country for them.

The elusive Shepherd's Hill is, I believe, near the site of the Ossett by-pass.

Another of our haunts nearer home was Flanshaw Beck, then surrounded by trees and fields. Our game was to swing across the water on a rope tied to a branch of an overhanging tree, the one falling in least being judged the winner. I, being the heaviest, elected to walk across the sewage pipe instead. I was told recently that Bettina was petrified at the thought of balancing but was pressurised into it to avoid being labelled a 'cissy'!

The most daring outing was this one:

31 May 1942 Today the Club cycled up Barnsley Road to swim in Woolley Dam. Kathleen provoked fear in all of us, swearing it was a bottomless pit. John ridiculed this and he and Beryl Gilbertson (who joined us for the day) swam across to prove it. Then cakes and lemonade at the little stall to take the edge off our hunger. Betti, in spite of being told by her mother not to go in a boat, joined us for a swift row across the lake.

There had been an ancient water mill served by an earlier dam. The dam we knew, a crescent-shaped lake, had been designed in 1766 by James Brindley for the then owner of Woolley Hall, Godfrey Wentworth. It was drained in the early 1950s.[3]

Our parties were famous too. The Minute Book records our anniversary one on 6 September 1941 when, as it says, 'Amici et Comites Clari' lived up to their name. The central event was a treasure hunt in Poplar Avenue, organised by Margaret, Betti and

myself, which involved (among other activities), scrambling blindfold
on an obstacle race, unravelling strings to reach further stages of the
hunt, passing through an Air Raid shelter where Betti was disguised
as a ghost, climbing pipes and finally locating the treasure down a
manhole. It was Kathleen who recovered it. Later 'some Amici played
Dooking (sic) for apples and others were bored.' The party ended at
the Olsons with games and dancing, 'Kathleen being expert at
Tangos'. Another party followed just before Christmas:

> *20 December 1941. Today was the day of the party. Pearl and John,
> who arrived late, were met with six gloomy faces and an unchanged
> CV (the Choir Vestry). It seemed that Derek and JP had jumped out
> of the cupboard shouting 'A Merry Christmas' 'And a Happy New
> Year' just when Mr. Hazel, choirmaster, was in the room.*[4] *The ticking
> off which ensued, as well as the fact that the building was full of
> Guides, Brownies, Scouts and Footballers, and two weddings, had
> dragged the ACC down in the mire. However 'never say die', 'Amici
> etcetera' and the forms were cleared, mistletoe and holly hung and
> decorations slung around* (with no tacks). *The club played boxed
> noses and various tricks and soon Mr. Hazel reappeared. He was in a
> better mood and showed an interest in our music. After a lot of
> gadding about, tea was produced. And what a spread! Sandwiches,
> sausage rolls, scones, buns, tarts, cake, jellies and cider! Mr. Langley
> was invited to join us.* (It's just as well to be in with the right
> people.) *When he departed the eats were disposed of and the cider
> glopped. When all was cleared, the building was cleared and the
> caretaker left. Consequences were played and Derek and John startled
> the rest with a 'ghost'. Till 7.30, the club played Murders and
> Mistletoe and Sardines, and the last half hour was devoted to a gay,
> hilarious romp. During the evening the CV was visited by Mr. Hazel,
> Mr. Langley, a policeman and the vicar, and also a mysterious
> disappearing boy called Alan Auty. Win obliged with the piano and
> altogether it was a most enjoyable time. A long walk home and a visit
> to Wol, in which John trailed the tablecloth and Mar. lost her scarf,
> ended the evening.*

The Club invented a secret vocabulary of a dozen words and phrases:
glop – to eat and enjoy; marookish – mock serious; massive – great,
important, lovely; gink – a spoilsport; ginking – arguing, quarrelling;
resudicate – to work out, to analyse; young stag – good man, great
fellow; staggish – important; skipoosh – to hurry; slushy sandwiches
– salad and lots of salad cream; wossed – tired out. Many of these
words have survived in my family. My son and I resudicate when we

are organising; we glop when we eat hungrily; and slushy sandwiches are often made for summer teas in the garden.

Looking back amongst the leaves of the old Green File, I marvel at the imagination and resourcefulness of the members of the Amici of Poplar Avenue. We believed in discipline and order but we made our own amusements, played pranks and did daring things. We rationalised our fear of war by working for it financially. We were a mixture, childlike but sophisticated. Most of all we had understanding, caring parents who gave us ideas, encouraged us a bit, but were ever watchful.

The rest of the summer of 1942 was spent cycling, mostly to our old haunts, but also to Scout camps, taking jam and cakes to the boys. We all attended Lupset Church for Sunday Evensong, an attraction being the Youth Club dance in the Church Hall. Studying for exams also curtailed our meetings and expeditions. The ACC members grew up, still friends, in a golden early adolescence, thanks to understanding parents and loyalty to our Club and each other.

Notes and References

1. This was the area developed by George Crook and Sons in the 1930s, including Beechwood, Oakwood and Pinewood Avenues.
2. *Wakefield Express* 15 March 1991 Among the dead were two children,. five year old John Anthony Russell Topping and his younger brother Frederick Neil Topping, sons of James Frederick and Barbara Topping, 48 Thornes Road. Among others killed was Elsie Robertshaw, 50 Thornes Road
3. Woolley Dam was bought by the National Coal Board in 1949 but was leased to Frank Hopkinson, who maintained it as a recreational centre. In 1951 underground workings from Haigh Colliery came closer to the dam and a civil engineer, engaged to inspect it, gave an adverse report. It was drained in the autumn of 1951 to remove the threat to Newmillerdam village. *Wakefield Express,* 18.8.1952 and 3.11.1951.
4. G F Hazell, who lived at 343 Horbury Road, was appointed organist and choirmaster at St George's in 1940.

7. A FIELD IN BELLE VUE

by Peter I Wood

SINCE 1878 A GRASS FIELD situated in what was then the parish of Sandal[1] has been the venue for many sporting activities and much entertainment. When the field became Belle Vue, the home of Wakefield Trinity, the name began to be recognised amongst sporting organisations not only in England but in many countries throughout the world. There are, however, many non-sporting people who can look back to an event they either played a part in or witnessed there, and the name Belle Vue will conjure up their memories of those long-gone days.

For many years the roads to Belle Vue from town, on a Saturday afternoon from September to April, would be crowded with trams or, in later years, with red buses, and thronged with rushing crowds, all making their way to the football ground. The largest crowd ever seen there was on 26 March 1936 for a Rugby League Cup semi-final between Huddersfield and Leeds when over 37,900 packed the ground (although how many could have seen the match was another matter). Now public transport has given way to private cars, Saturday sport has become a Sunday event, and the crowds are much depleted. But the ground is still the home of Wakefield Trinity and the field is still available for any event that requires a flat area with banks for spectators.

It is not a field in which Rugby League alone has been played for it has been used for a variety of sports, entertainment and events at either parochial or county level, for many years. The field has had not only football boots trampling its grass but also the hooves of horses and sheep, paws of dogs, the footwear of many instrumentalists that have played there, and the plimsolls of thousands of children. Around the perimeter of the playing area cyclists and motor cyclists have raced, using the banked ends to maintain their momentum on the curves, and white lines quite alien to those of rugby have often marked the field. Now the future of the ground is in doubt for although Wakefield M D Council stated in early 1997 that the ground would always be a playing field, by August 1997, with the chance of both rugby codes going to a new ground at Durkar, the idea of 'superior' houses being built at Belle Vue was receiving Council support.

The football team Trinity gets its name from Holy Trinity Church which was built in 1840 and situated between Thornhill Gate and Kirkgate, where in 1873 members of its Young Men's Society formed a rugby team – which at that time meant Rugby Union (Figures 1 and 2). The young men of Holy Trinity Church were already capable of organising a sports day for in 1872 they held an 'Athletic Sports' on the Ings and had the band of the Fifth West Yorkshire Royal Volunteers entertaining the spectators.[2] The first matches of this fledgling football club were played on one of the flatter areas at Heath Common, not on the field used for athletics at Ings Road and where Pinderfields Clarence Athletic Club held their sports days. The 1877 season saw Trinity using a field, admission 2d, which was described as 'being adjacent to Mr Hepworth's organ manufactory'[3] and was behind the newly-built *Alexandra Hotel* where the players

Figure 1. Holy Trinity Church which was opened in 1841 and where the football team was founded in 1873.

Figure 2. Wakefield Trinity football team, 1875

changed. This field was only a stop-gap measure as for the 1878-79 season the players moved to the present ground across the road (Figure 3). It was here on 19 April that Trinity, after their success against the Kirkstall team[4], played against Birch in a charity match and handed £37 12s 3d to Clayton Hospital.

Trinity's stength on the football field can be clearly seen for they had the confidence to visit Ireland in January 1882 to play two matches. At Lansdowne Road they defeated Dublin by one try and two touch-downs to one dead ball. In Belfast they played against Northern Ireland and drew at four minor points each. In the autumn, Dublin made the return match, much to the pleasure of the people of Wakefield.[5] Other visitors to Belle Vue in those Rugby Union days were Cambridge University, Blackheath and United Hospitals, Swansea, Cardiff and Newport. Local clubs were represented by Manningham from Bradford, Leeds St John's, Leeds Parish Church, Brighouse Rangers, Horbury, Wakefield Albion, Wakefield St. Austin's, Thornes, Stanley, and another club playing in Belle Vue. In December 1892 the Wakefield Trinity Football and Athletic Club (as there was already a Trinity Athletic Club and those members must have felt that they should enjoy any new facilities) agreed to lease the field.[6] This field, part of the Bird Bush estate, began at Doncaster Road and took in the land now occupied by the Conservative Club[7] and an old cinema[8] plus the unmade road

Figure 3. An aerial view of Wakefield Trinity's ground at Belle Vue on 21 March 1936 when it had a record crowd of 37,906 for the cup semi-final between Huddersfield and Leeds. Receipts were £2,456 10s 5d. Courtesy the Directors of Wakefield Trinity RL Club.

between the church, the cinema and the club. At the Agbrigg end the field extended to part way down the present St Catherine's Street. It had been bought by Jonathan Haigh for £6,000 from the Governors of the Wakefield Charities in 1877. The field could have been larger but the Ecclesiastical Commissioners had already transferred land bought from the Governors of the Wakefield Charities on the eastern side for St.Catherine's School and then the church.[9] There was also a large plot of land by the side of Agbrigg maltkilns and at the end of St Catherine's School which was not used by Trinity but which at one time served as a grass pitch for the school.

Wakefield Trinity was an athletic club as well as a football one. By 1879 it had transferred its annual festival of Wakefield Trinity Athletic Club from Ings Road to the more up-market College Grove cricket ground where the sports would remain for the next twenty years. That year, 1879, the prizes amounted to £100 in value for the eleven races, but they were for members only. Athletics being an amateur sport at the time, the winners could not accept cash prizes but only articles of a personal or domestic nature such as dessert knives, tea and coffee services, inkstands, card trays, etc.

The profits from the 1892 meeting were set aside and would, after other fund raising, be used to purchase the Belle Vue field. Three years later the purchase price was reached and in 1895 a resolution was passed that the club should acquire the field. It became the property of Trinity in September 1896. The committee, on behalf of the members, offered shares to form a limited company and so Wakefield Trinity Athletic Club became unique in the Union and later Rugby League world. Haigh, who was a vice-president of the Club, received £2,800 and £1,200 in shares, for the field.

The pitch had been surrounded by a wire fence; then a sacking screen was put round the ground but this must have been difficult to maintain and easy to damage if one did not want to pay for admission. The screen was replaced, as cash became available, with a wooden fence of railway sleepers some of which, at the St Catherine's Street end, were still in place in the 1960s.

Viewing the matches could have been difficult for latecomers as there was no terracing at this time and the field containing the playing area was much larger so that even standing on the touchline the spectators were much futher from the playing area than one would be today. The northern end of the field came to within a few feet of the St Catherine's Church's southern boundary wall and it was much later that both church and Trinity agreed to the ginnel which separates the two (Figure 4). One the eastern side of the ground was a row of seats that stretched the full length of the field. Seats were built also at either side of a small stand on the west side and continued around the corners towards the goal posts. This stand had been built by 1890, which must be an indication of Trinity's long-term hopes for the ground as at that time they were still leasing the field.

During the close season of 1895 some of the northern clubs met at Huddersfield to discuss the payment to their players for time they had to take off work. The Rugby Union authorities would not allow such payment in their amateur game and so the game split into Union and League. Trinity played their first game under the new code against Bradford, but the sides still retained the fifteen players.[10]

Land at St Catherine's Street end was sold to local builders and entrepreneurs in 1896[11] enabling the club to make many improvements which were carried out during the close season of 1898. The field was levelled so there was now no slope to the playing area. A first-class cycle track with banked ends, though not as high as the present ends, was laid around the outside of the pitch which was surrounded by iron railings. There was now a terrace from which 10,000 to 12,000 spectators could see the whole playing area. The improvements made Belle Vue one of the best grounds in rugby and athletics. Lord Milton, the Liberal-Unionist member of Parliament for Wakefield officially declared the reconstituted ground open for the opening match of the season on 24 September 1898, with Trinity losing to Halifax.

There was one small wooden stand of only twenty yards length on the eastern side which was demolished and replaced by the covered terrace in 1926. The small grandstand on the western side came down to the field edge but was later reconstructed. Plans had been prepared to make it much larger and in 1898 the front was removed and the paddock was dug out and stepped. The stand completed by

Figure 4. St. Catherine's Church, Doncaster Road, with the railings of the football ground behind it, 1998. *Kate Taylor.*

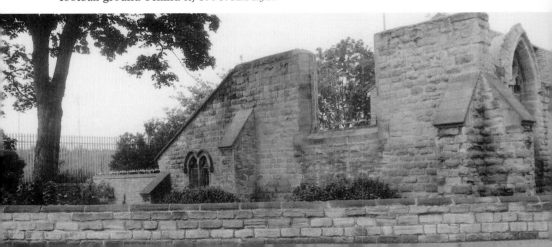

July of that year was still basically a wooden structure with glass ends
but underneath had been constructed baths, dressing rooms, offices
and a forty-foot long refreshment saloon at the end towards the
church. For many years it was from this stand that the players took
the field, although it was improved in 1932. It was used as an air-raid
shelter during the Second World War for the children of St
Catherine's School.[12]

The twenty-ninth annual Athletic Festival was held again at
College Grove but from the following year, 1899, Trinity's athletic
sports took place at their own ground at Belle Vue.

Earlier that year, at a meeting held in the Royal Hotel, it was
agreed that the Wakefield Trinity Athletic Company should have a
section called the Cycling and Athletic Section of Wakefield Trinity
Athletic Club. Obviously the club had enough members wanting to
use the cycling track and facilities now that some £6,000 had been
spent on ground improvements. The aim of this new section was to
promote afternoon, evening and monthly meetings, similar to the
programme of Leeds Cycling and Athletic Club. Two committees
were formed, one for each section. Training tickets were issued at five
shillings, inclusive of membership which would entitle the member to
admission to the ground and the use of dressing rooms and baths
under the proposed new stand.

The Cycling Committee was now able to promote, in August
1899, the Yorkshire Road Club's 100-mile paced race around the
ground for the twenty-five guineas challenge vase.

The club was still not satisfied with the facilities they could offer
and the profits of the thirty-third annual Athletic Meeting, held in
1902, were ear-marked to give the ground, the sportsmen and the
spectators the required improvements. Possibly one of the items
purchased was a grass-cutting machine for there had been a time
when the club had advertised letting the field for sheep grazing
during the close season. By 30 July a programme of sports had been
arranged:

100 yards handicap	3 prizes to the total value of £13 13s
200 yards handicap	3 prizes to the total value of £6 16s
440 yards handicap	3 prizes to the total value of £8 18s
1 mile handicap	3 prizes to the total value of £8 18s
1 mile bicycle	3 prizes to the total value of £10 10s
2 mile bicycle	3 prizes to the total value of £13 13s
another 2 mile bicycle	3 prizes to the total value of £6 16s

(this was open only to people resident within six miles of Wakefield

Cathedral)
The final event was 440 yards handicap (members in football kit)
3 prizes to the total value of £4 14s 6d.

Spectators would be able to listen to the Rutland Mills Band and watch a Grand Gymnastic Exhibition provided by members of the Leeds Gymnasium.

An extra for the festival that year was a five-mile motor-bike race around the cycle track which had been specially prepared and inspected for this event. With a membership of over 500 it is not surprising that there would be some young men eager to show their skills in such a manner.[13]

The improvements to the ground were such that the Rugby Union staged the Yorkshire Cup Final between Skipton and Castleford in 1903 followed by the Wallabies against Yorkshire on their tour of 1908.

That would seem to be the end of Union at Belle Vue but not so. A match between Wakefield RU and Sandal RU was played in 1936. In October 1943 a Northern Command English and Welsh 15 played against a Scottish 15. During the interval a team of Irish Guards pulled against a team from the Royal Scots in a three-pull tug of war.

The amateur status of players, it was feared, could be contaminated by playing on professionals' pitches. A directive from the Rugby Union in 1902 in answer to a request for a Union match to be played at Belle Vue, stated that the ground was the property of Wakefield Trinity Athetic Club and Trinity (Rugby League) were only the tenants so there was no danger to the true amateur.[14]

Another game played by the members of the Athletic Club was La Crosse, and, judging by the number of members selected for county and international honours, Trinity had a strong team. Not only did they have a successful side - they won the Yorkshire County Flag Competition when they beat Leeds twice - but in the Yorkshire team of 1882 against Cheshire there were six Trinity players in the winning team. Two players were picked for the England v Ireland match and C E Bartram, Trinity's Football Assistant Secretary, scored one of the goals although the team lost by four goals to three.

Since athletics had always been of prime importance to Trinity it was no surprise that in 1909 a one-mile race for £100 was organised between thirty-five year old Oliver Littlewood and Joe Taylor of South Hiendley, a Trinity forward. 2,287 people paid over £64 to watch the expected four-lap race. Taylor won when Littlewood

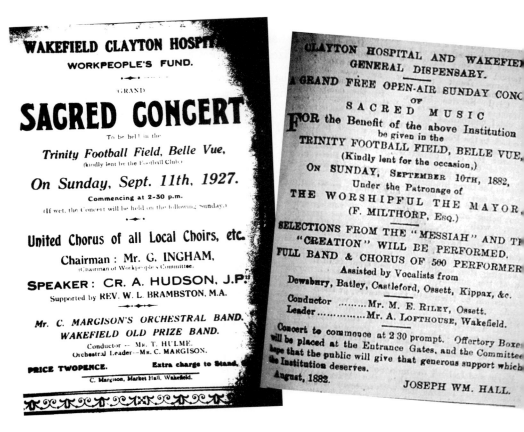

Figure 5. Programme cover for a Sacred Concert in 1927. Sunday entertainment was frowned on by members of the clergy but perhaps the notion that the items were 'sacred' made it acceptable. Earlier concerts were free, with offertory boxes placed at the gates, but by 1927 an entry fee was charged. *Wakefield Library Headquarters.*

limped off at the three-quarter mile post. He had been more successful in 1898 when, against thirty runners in an 880-yard race, he had come joint first.

There are many examples of the Belle Vue field being used to raise money for charities. In 1882 Trinity played Cheetham with the ground receipts of £35 2s 5d going to the Clayton Hospital and General Dispensary Hospital Saturday fund. The same year Trinity married players were against Trinity single players with the receipts again going to the hospital and victory to the single men. The largest charity events staged at Belle Vue must have been the Concerts of

Sacred Music. (Figure 5) The first was organised in 1882 with choirs from Dewsbury, Castleford, Ossett, Kippax and elsewhere under the leadership of A Lofthouse and M E Riley. Although the proceeds were to go to the hospital there was strong opposition from various religious leaders in the local community for the concert was to be performed on a Sunday.[15] The children of the Sunday Schools did not seem to share their spiritual leaders' opinion for it was later reported that at one school only thirty-three children had attended out of 400 regular members and at another only nine of the usual 200. This first of many annual concerts had 480 vocalists and seventy instrumentalists. It was estimated that there were between 17,000 and 25,000 spectators at this rare Sunday entertainment. There were only four policemen on duty to control the huge crowd, Superintendent Hall the Deputy Chief Constable, Sergeant Wetherall of Belle Vue and two constables. As well as the masses that turned out for the concert music, the Mayor and Mayoress of Wakefield, several Aldermen, and members of the gentry also came to listen and swell the proceeds to £112 11s.

At the beginning of the twentieth century, with trade depression and unemployment, leading citizens were concerned over the footwear of the children. There are many reports in school log books regarding children's absences in bad weather due to poor footwear, or the absence of it. Pontefract had 'Boots for Bairns' and Wakefield had the 'Poor Children's Boot Fund'. Leading Wakefield's fund was the Chief Constable, T M Harris, aided by other police officers. A match was played at Belle Vue between the police and Old Trinity, bringing in the handsome amount of about £70 which would have purchased many pairs of boots.

When Sandal and Belle Vue organised a charity carnival in May 1909 the field was used for the sports after the 'Monstre Procession', led by the Dreadnoughts and Wakefield City Brass Band and an elected 'king' and 'queen', had wound through both villages. It cost 9d to watch the sports and entertainment and have tea; children, who might have eaten less, paid 3d. The charities benefited by £12.

The ground was used by Buffalo Bill's Wild West Show, then touring England, on 9 October 1903. (Figure 6) The show arrived filling four special trains, with 500 horses and 800 performers, a hundred of which were supposed to be Red Indians led by Chief Long Wolf.[16] Colonel Cody entertained with an attack on the Deadwood Stage, an exhibition of mounted warriors from around the world, Roosevelt's Rough Riders, trick shooting and much more.

Footballers who played at Belle Vue were not always the 'pros'.

With so many amateur players in works and public house teams at the turn of the century it was not long before Trinity promoted a cup. The Works Cup Competition, for teams within six miles of Wakefield Cathedral, started in 1903. Each round and the final were played at the Belle Vue ground. Of the firms taking part in that first competition only J Rhodes and Son remains today; Manor, Lofthouse, Woolley and Parkhill Collieries have gone with pit closures; George Craddock and Co, Calder Vale Boiler Works and E Green and Son have gone in closures and amalgamations. The winning team gained the cup and gold medals; there were silver medals for the runners-up.

There have been at least two football matches at Belle Vue that have been very different from the normal game. In 1892 the ground was host to a match between Wakefield's Tradesmen and Zaro's Circus Troupe. Zaro, or James Comerford, performed with his company from 1891 in the People's Empire in Teall Street.[17] The players of both sides wore fancy dress and the score did not matter. The other memorable match was played on 20 October 1906 and was known as the Belle Vue Riot. It was between Trinity Reserves and Sharlston Rovers in the Dewsbury and Wakefield League. The referee had taken the names of two Rovers' players and send off a third when fighting erupted between players and spectators. Bruce of Sharlston was hit and knocked out by a corner post wielded by some person after he, Bruce, had tried to stop Dawson from being hit with the same post. The police were called and cleared the pitch. According to the press the assailant was recognised but not reported to the police to allow him time to 'own up'.

On 12 January 1922 a game was played which would have brought the 'young bloods' of Wakefield

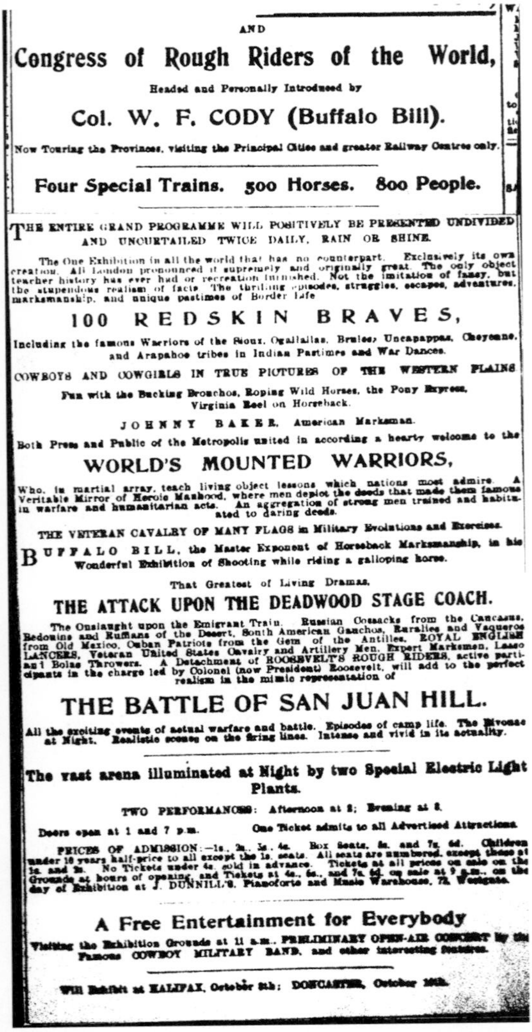

AND

Congress of Rough Riders of the World,

Headed and Personally Introduced by

Col. W. F. CODY (Buffalo Bill).

Now Touring the Provinces, visiting the Principal Cities and greater Railway Centres only.

Four Special Trains. 500 Horses. 800 People.

THE ENTIRE GRAND PROGRAMME WILL POSITIVELY BE PRESENTED UNDIVIDED AND UNCURTAILED TWICE DAILY, RAIN OR SHINE.

The One Exhibition in all the world that has no counterpart. Exclusively its own creation. All London pronounced it supremely and originally great. The only object teacher history has ever had or recreation furnished. Not the imitation of fancy, but the stupendous realism of facts. The thrilling episodes, struggles, escapes, adventures, marksmanship, and unique pastimes of Border Life

100 REDSKIN BRAVES,

Including the famous Warriors of the Sioux, Ogallallas, Brules, Uncapappas, Cheyenne, and Arapahoe tribes in Indian Pastimes and War Dances.

COWBOYS AND COWGIRLS IN TRUE PICTURES OF THE WESTERN PLAINS

Fun with the Bucking Bronchos, Roping Wild Horses, the Pony Express, Virginia Reel on Horseback.

JOHNNY BAKER, American Marksman.

Both Press and Public of the Metropolis united in according a hearty welcome to the

WORLD'S MOUNTED WARRIORS,

Who, in martial array, teach living object lessons which nations most admire. A Veritable Mirror of Heroic Manhood, where men depict the deeds that made them famous in warfare and humanitarian acts. An aggregation of strong men trained and habituated to daring deeds.

THE VETERAN CAVALRY OF MANY FLAGS in Military Evolutions and Exercises.

BUFFALO BILL, the Master Exponent of Horseback Marksmanship, in his Wonderful Exhibition of Shooting while riding a galloping horse.

That Greatest of Living Dramas,

THE ATTACK UPON THE DEADWOOD STAGE COACH.

The Onslaught upon the Emigrant Train. Russian Cossacks from the Caucasus, Bedouins and Ruffians of the Desert, South American Gauchos, Ruralies and Vaqueros from Old Mexico, Cuban Patriots from the Gem of the Antilles, ROYAL ENGLISH LANCERS, Veteran United States Cavalry and Artillery Men, Expert Marksmen, Lasso and Bolas Throwers. A Detachment of ROOSEVELT'S ROUGH RIDERS, active participants in the charge led by Colonel (now President) Roosevelt, will add to the perfect realism in the mimic representation of

THE BATTLE OF SAN JUAN HILL.

All the exciting events of actual warfare and battle. Episodes of camp life. The Bivouac at Night. Realistic scenes on the firing lines. Intense and vivid in its actuality.

The vast arena illuminated at Night by two Special Electric Light Plants.

TWO PERFORMANCES: Afternoon at 2; Evening at 8.

Doors open at 1 and 7 p.m. One Ticket admits to all Advertised Attractions.

PRICES OF ADMISSION:—1s., 2s., 3s., 4s. Box Seats, 5s. and 7s. 6d. Children under 10 years half-price to all except the 1s. seats. All seats are numbered, except those at 1s. and 2s. No Tickets under 4s. sold in advance. Tickets at all prices on sale on the Grounds at hours of opening, and Tickets at 4s., 5s., and 7s. 6d. on sale at 9 a.m., on the day of Exhibition at J. DUNNILL'S, Pianoforte and Music Warehouse, 7a, Westgate.

A Free Entertainment for Everybody

Visiting the Exhibition Grounds at 11 a.m., PRELIMINARY OPEN-AIR CONCERT by the Famous COWBOY MILITARY BAND, and other interesting features.

Will Exhibit at HALIFAX, October 8th; DONCASTER, October 10th.

Figure 6. An advertisement from The *Wakefield Express* for Buffalo Bill's Wild West Show on 9 October 1903.

flocking to the ground. Dick Kerr's Ladies played against Hey's Brewery (Bradford) Ladies in a Ladies' championship (Figure 7). Dick Kerr had Madame Carmen Pomies, the French international half-back in their world champion team, but Hey's were the Yorkshire champions, so they must have been good! Again the proceeds were for Wakefield and District hospitals.

Soccer was played at the ground during the 1930s. These matches became an annual event between Wakefield City Police and Halifax Borough Police and were played in late winter or early spring. The 1933 game was on a snow-covered pitch with Halifax winning by five goals to one. That was before the days of white footballs.

The other sport not usually associated with Belle Vue took place in 1936 when an exhibition game of baseball was played by Wakefield Cubs organised by R B Graham. The event was part of a nationwide scheme to promote baseball into the national game.

There had always been good relations between St Catherine's Church and School and the football club.[18] In 1892 the church used the field for a Grand Fete and Gala to raise funds for the enlargement of the school. The school often used the field for their sports day and annual treats which were carried out in a flamboyant manner with the Belle Vue Brass Band leading the hymn singing before launching into their own programme of music.[19]

For the sixtieth anniversary of Queen Victoria's reign, chidren of Sandal, Milnthorpe and Belle Vue, together with the over-sixties, enjoyed a tea, games and races at the ground.

On 1 September 1909 the Wakefield elementary schools met at the ground for an afternoon of sports and folk-dancing with children from Clarendon Street School demonstrating maypole dancing. As at all big occasions members of the St John Ambulance were in attendance but that had only one accident, when a boy fell from the railings he was climbing and broke a collar bone. A similar event of children's dancing was organised in July 1953 to celebrate Queen Elizabeth's coronation.

The field was used by Wakefield Agricultural Society for their

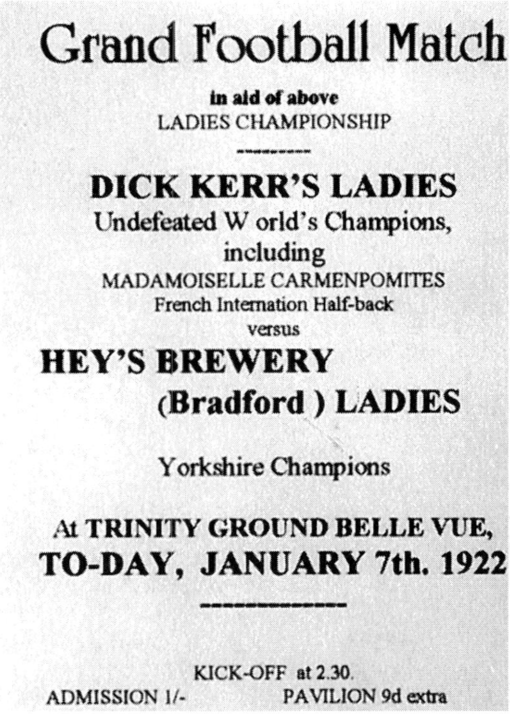

Figure 7. An advertisement from *The Wakefield Express* for a ladies championship football match.

Grand Football Match

In aid of above
LADIES CHAMPIONSHIP

DICK KERR'S LADIES
Undefeated World's Champions,
including
MADAMOISELLE CARMENPOMITES
French Internation Half-back
versus

HEY'S BREWERY
(Bradford) LADIES

Yorkshire Champions

At **TRINITY GROUND BELLE VUE,**
TO-DAY, JANUARY 7th. 1922

KICK-OFF at 2.30.
ADMISSION 1/-   PAVILION 9d extra

THIS DAY (SATURDAY).

THE Annual SHOW of HORSES and DOGS
Will be held in the
TRINITY FOOTBALL FIELD,
Belle Vue, Wakefield,
TO-DAY (SATURDAY), JULY 12TH.
The entry of Horses and noted Dogs is a large one.

SPECIAL ATTRACTIONS:
Horses in Harness, 2 lots of HURDLE LEAPERS,
and a mile HURDLE RACE by Ponies.
A well-known PRIZE BRASS BAND will be in attendance.

ADMISSION:—11 to 3, One Shilling; after 3, Sixpence.
C. J. DODDS, Sec.

THE WAKEFIELD AGRICULTURAL SOCIET
21ST ANNUAL SHOW AND GALA will be
held in the TRINITY FOOTBALL FIELD, BELLE V
Wakefield, on SATURDAY NEXT, June 1st.

THE SHOW will consist of HORS
HURDLE-LEAPING. TROTTING, by c
brated Horses; Pony, and Donkey Racing, als
splendid collection of DOGS, POULTRY, PIGEO
and RABBITS.
Mr. UTTLEY, of the Royal Hotel, Norton, wil
in attendance with his renowned PERFORMI
DONKEY "Shamrock" and PONY "Wee John
10½ hands. The Donkey won the £5 5s. Cup at Ha
in 1894, and the £10 Prize at Doncaster Circus
November, 1894, beating Mr. Boswell's celebr
Jumping Pony (Oxford), and the performance of th
two animals will repay a visit to the Show.
A GALA in the Evening from 6 to 9 o'clock.
The DEWSBURY OLD PRIZE BAND will b
attendance.
Refreshments on the Ground.
ADMISSION: 11 to 2, 1s.; 2 to 6, 6d.; and 6 to 9
the Gala), 3d.
C. J. DODDS, Secreta

Figure 8. Two advertisements from *The Wakefield Express* for annual shows organised by Wakefield Agricultural Society.

annual show as early as 1892 (Figure 8). In that year there were a dog hurdle-leaping competition, pony racing and horse displays. The show boasted of a Great Special Show of roses and plants with a military band to provide musical entertainment. The 1895 show had 914 entries including 150 horses, 299 dogs, 199 poultry and 119 mice. The groundsman may not have been pleased to have had the playing area cut up with the hooves of horses and ponies, but the pitch would not have been lawn like the surface of the 1960s when the Bingley Turf Research Centre was often called in for advice to make the field into a prime grass playing surface.

Many people will remember the film, from Wakefield-born David Storey's book, *This Sporting Life* with Richard Harris in the leading role and with many of the successful 1962-3 players involved in the football scenes (Figure 9). These scenes were acted over and over on the field until the action looked real. During the close period when tickets were put on sale for the oncoming season several fans were puzzled on entering the ground to find that there were many groups of 'supporters' already in the ground. These cut-out groups may have swelled the crowd for some of the home matches but in no way did they contribute to the encouraging cheers!

The past few years have seen the Mela at Belle Vue. The strong local Asian community organised this getting together in 1994 and again in 1995. For their Mela in 1996 they used the field where, with events and stalls, Asians from towns and cities throughout Yorkshire enjoyed meeting friends and being entertained in the sunshine, with the proceeds going to Wakefield Hospice and the Imran

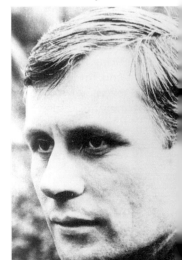

Figure 9. Wakefield-born novelist and playwright David Storey, author of *This Sporting Life* which drew on his own experiences as a Rugby player.

Khan Cancer Hospital. Two weeks later Trinity's committee ignored football for a short time when they organised a Caribbean party day to run along with the Trinity and Huddersfield match.

There is now (January 1998) talk of League and Union having one ground near the proposed Yorkshire County Cricket headquarters on Denby Dale Road. But the ground at Belle Vue has been an integral part of the community of Belle Vue, Agbrigg, Sandal and Wakefield, providing excitement and happiness to those thousands who have passed through its gates and one can only hope that it may continue to do so.

Sources

The Wakefield Express
The Wakefield and West Riding Herald
The Wakefield Herald
Wakefield City Council Minutes
Material in the John Goodchild Collection
Armitage, D W, and Lindley J C, Dreadnoughts: *A History of Wakefield Trinity F.C. 1873-1960 (1960)*.
Lindley, J C, 100 Years of Rugby: *The HIstory of Wakefield Trinity Football Club 1873-1973, (1973)*.

Notes and References

1. The first naming of the area as Belle Vue is a sale of land in 1876, but Belle Vue House (now the site of the cemetery) is on the 1800 Sandal Inclosure Map.
2. Advertisement in the *Wakefield Herald*, 7 September 1872.
3. Hepworth's works were at the corner of Clarion and Elm Tree Streets.
4. Leeds.
5. A report of the arrival of the Irish team in Wakefield and of the matches is in the *Wakefield Express*, 28 January 1882.
6. At the time of the Sandal Inclosure of 1800 the area belonged to Thomas Barraclough.
7. Built in 1895 as a tin hut.
8. Known variously as Trinity Picture Palace, Belle Vue Palace and the Palace Cosy Cinema, the picture house was built for Stephen Askew and opened on 7 November 1914.
9. The school was built in 1971 and the church consecrated in 1876.
10. The number did not fall to thirteen players until 1906.
11. Most of the land was purchased by J Elvey or Regent Street. His company became part of Elvey, Steele and Brooke. Four plots were bought by W Ash who had the maltkilns where the Superbowl now is. The street is now called Trinity Street.
11. The school never had any air-raid shelter other than the basement of the stand.
13. There were 502 registered members in 1903, still using Holly Lodge as a central meeting place. Holly Lodge was in Rodney Yard and had been acquired as a club room in 1884.
14. *Wakefield Express*, 6 September 1902
15. The most vociferous were Rev J R Wolstenholme from Zion, Rev Straton vicar of Wakefield, and Rev Hurt of St Helen's, Sandal.
16. His body was returned for re-burial in his tribe's hunting lands in 1997.
17. Taylor, C M P, *Right Royal: Wakefield Theatre 1776-1994*, (1995), pp 178-9. The entertainment would be classed today as an equestrian show rather than a circus.
18. D W Armitage was the school's headmaster and a long-serving committee member.
19. A most successful band in its day, but it failed to reappear after the Great War.

8. Bastardy in Ossett in the Early Nineteenth Century

by Ann Barnes

THIS STUDY WAS INSPIRED by the availability of two interesting primary sources and has been confined largely to the period 1800-1821 because of their nature.

There is considerable difficulty in determining the extent of bastardy. The reliability or consistency of recording a birth or baptism as that of an illegitimate child must, by the very nature of things, vary from time to time. Although statistical techniques have been devised to try to establish the reliability and consistency of the data, these are mostly of use in large-scale studies. A number of these have been conducted and their published results indicate trends in bastardy over periods of up to 400 years. These studies also seek to explain, largely in socio-econonic terms, fluctuations in the numbers of bastards. I have not sought to explain my findings but merely to report on what appears to have existed in the case of Ossett and to compare this with the findings of other researchers in similar fields.

Ossett, in the heart of the industrial West Riding, grew from 3,424 inhabitants in 1801 to 4,775 by 1821. It was a town of textile mills, of hand-loom weavers and a burgeoning coal industry, predominantly working class with few middle-class inhabitants. Its Overseers of the Poor seem to have been kept pretty busy. Large numbers claimed Outdoor Relief; even larger numbers claimed occasional help – records show disbursements for a midwife's services, for a funeral and even – though probably illegally – for a marriage! But bastardy seems to have been a major preoccupation for these gentlemen, although it has been suggested that such a preoccupation is more apparent than real[1]. They examined the erring woman and recorded every detail: It was gotten on a Sunday afternoon whilst the rest of the family were at church....in the chamber...with his boots on. (This is taken from an examination just outside my time-period.) The Ossett incumbent, Reverend Oliver Levey Collins, commented in 1841, Bastardy is sadly too common; but I have not so many to baptize as formerly. They look on it as a misfortune and not as a crime.

In the spring of 1821 the two Overseers of the Poor for the

township of Ossett cum Gawthorpe received the official communication requiring them to take a census of the township; they were asked to obtain details of the families therein and, only if it could be done without inconvenience, to note the ages of the various inhabitants. The surviving census listings are contained in two manuscript books compiled by the enumerators which are in two sections (Appendix 1): one names heads of households and numbers the dwellings, states how many families were present and gives the numbers of individuals in two specified occupational groups, agriculture and manufacturing, and how many in other occupations. No addresses are given. The other section lists males on the left and females on the right, with their ages, and columns labelled 0-5, 5-10, 10-15, 15-20, 20-30 etc. (again males on the left and females on the right, an arrangement which occasionally causes confusion about whose children are being recorded) in which numbers are entered to indicate the ages and genders of children. (An immediate problem occurs here in that the ages of 5, 10, 15 etc. are not exclusive and individuals of these ages could be entered in either of two columns.) The names of the children are not generally given but an exception seems to be made when the children are not in the same household as their parents – numbers of apprentices and servants who live in, and children, where living with people outside the possible age-range of their parents, are named. However this crude rule of thumb has its exceptions too.

The enumerators were certainly not asked to comment on the legitimacy or otherwise of the offspring, but they did. Some 126 minors are denoted as 'illegitimate'.

One major problem with this source is that the relationships between individuals are not stated, so estimates (along the lines of those devised for the 1841 census, which suffers from the same omission) of probable relationships have to be made, and although it is possible to determine many of these with reasonable confidence, nevertheless a small number remain intractable. Another major difficulty lies with the enumerator, whose imperfect knowledge, value judgments, personal prejudices, or other failures have caused anomalies in this data source: some who would be, and would have been at the time, generally regarded as legitimate are labelled otherwise and vice versa. The labelling process seems to break down as the children get older. This could be a product of the enumerator's failing memory, an indication that he was comparatively new to the post/area, or that the 'condition' had been 'outgrown' or 'spent' as the child evolves from a burden on the rates into a productive member of society. However communities have been found elsewhere where individuals aged up to forty-nine are still labelled as illegitimate.[2]

A bundle of Ossett Poor Law Administration papers survives, most important among which for this study is the Bastardy Book kept by the Overseers and which records the name of the mother, of the putative father, the date of the Bastardy Order and the weekly rate of pay. (Figure 1) Surprisingly the sex of the child is not recorded although a Bastardy Order would not have been legal without it, nor is the date of birth given.[3] Bastardy Orders were made against the alleged fathers of illegitimate children to ensure that they contributed to the maintenance of their offspring (Figure 2). The fathers' payments to the Overseer or his clerk, to indemnify the costs to the township, are recorded. So too are comments indicating the death of the child, father or mother, the father being imprisoned or going away, and other facts deemed relevant. Of course only those cases where a Bastardy Order has been obtained are recorded; cases where the putative father has remained elusive, or where the child is not, or is not likely to become, chargeable to the township are not recorded.

The book starts in 1797 and continues to about 1819, when some of the accounts indicate that they have been carried forward to a new book which seems not to have survived. Three births between 1797 and 1799 are listed here in order to complete the data relating to specific women who were producing bastards also within the period 1800-1821.

Other papers in this Poor Law bundle include Removal Orders, lists of Township Apprentices, one or two Bastardy Orders not included in the Bastardy Book, some examinations, and some thin booklets, possibly Overseers Account Books but, in appearance, rather informal and ephemeral, which record Outdoor Relief payments, under headings of By pay, Child pay and rents etc. An undated Militia list survives in the same archive (the John Goodchild Collection), which lists all men aged 18-45 with details of their age, occupation, number of dependent children, and whether they were disqualified from serving by infirmity or other reason. This list has been dated provisionally to between 1810 and 1812, but extensive comparison with the 1821 census now suggests a probable date of 1809. Unfortunately the document is somewhat decayed and not all of the 228 names are legible. Of those that are, only a small number can be correlated with those of the putative fathers. The 1807 Poll Book, containing the names of seventy-six Ossett men, rather more predictably yields even fewer relevant men.

The Ossett Methodist Chapel baptisms do not include any children who were labelled or who can be identified as illegitimate, but this is hardly surprising in view of strict Methodist attitudes to fornication. Ossett Green Congregationalist Chapel baptisms include twenty-two bastards, identified by a variety of terms: bastard, baseborn, illegitimate, natural child or simply as the child of two named parents with different surnames, or identified as the child of a mother only. This record is particularly interesting and useful because it gives the date of birth as well as of baptism, and usually names the putative father. Ossett was, at the time in question, part of the parish of Dewsbury, but from 1792 a chapel of ease in Ossett had conducted baptisms. Unfortunately many of the pages of the register prior to January 1813 are so totally illegible that they have not even been microfilmed (thus it has not been possible to calculate even the crudest bastardy ratios for those years) and of those which are on microfilm, many are still not decipherable. Nevertheless we can find 124 bastards identified, usually by the description natural child. Unfortunately most of these records fail to give the date of birth, nor are the putative fathers named, although two of the children are given what may be the father's surname.

The 1822 Baines (Trade) Directory added little further relevevant information.

It is perhaps desirable to outline some of the more relevant points of law relating to bastardy and the workings of the Poor Law at the time. Lord Coke is quoted as saying 'We term all by the name of bastards that are born out of lawful marriage'.[4] A bastard was chargeable to the parish in which it was born, irrespective of its mother's – or father's – settlement; hence the urgent removal of

Figure 1. Pages from the Ossett Bastardy Book. *The John Goodchild Collection.*

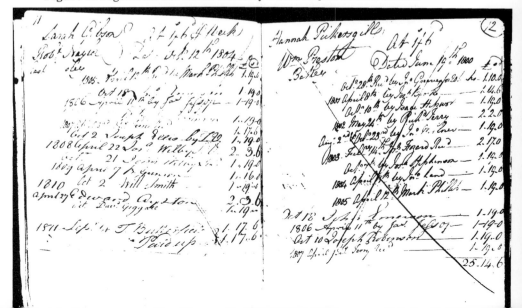

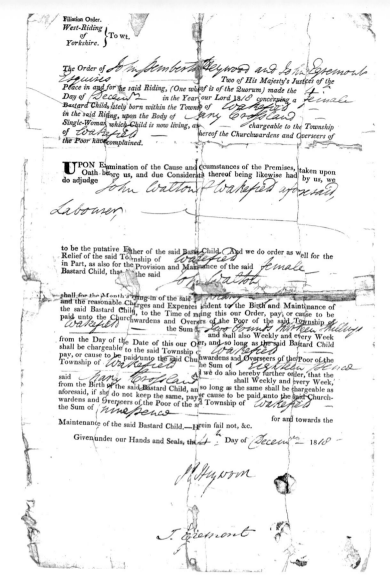

Figure 2. A bastardy order issued in Wakefield on 4 December 1818 requiring John Walton, labourer, of Wakefield, to pay an immediate £2 15s and a regular eighteenpence a week thereafter for the maintenance of the female child born to Mary Crossland. *Wakefield Library Headquarters.*

pregnant spinsters from a township. Of sixty-four Removal Orders to and from Ossett during the period under consideration eleven (17.8%) definitely related to pregnant spinsters and a further nine almost certainly did so, making 31 percent. The term 'settlement' refers to the parish, or township, where an individual had a right to poor relief if this was needed. In the first instance one's settlement lay in the place where one was born. This might be superceded by the place where one had held an apprenticeship or the place to which one had removed and lived as a ratepayer. A Bastardy Order could not be obtained until after the child was born ('No child is a bastard until it is born' [5]) and only then if it was likely to become chargeable to the parish, although it has been pointed out that it is self-evident that every bastard is likely to become so.[6] The Order was to indemnify the parish only for as long as the child was chargeable. If the child died, or acquired a settlement elsewhere, the father would be discharged from any further monetary obligation. Contrary to the view that the Orders normally last until the child was old enough to maintain itself, Ossett Orders seem to have been made for seven years only and the mother would have to filiate again after that period. Few seem to have done so.

All these sources have been entered into one comprehensive database, detailing every identified bastardy event in Ossett between the chosen dates, together with all known data about each event. This forms Appendix 2. Columns record, wherever possible, the mother's name and her age, if given in the 1821 census enumerators' books, together with her approximate age at the birth of that particular child where this can be deduced. The date of any Bastardy Order is given and the date of the baptism, the child's name or gender, and the putative father's name together with his age and occupation (from the Militia List – ML; Poll Book -PB; or the census listing -CL). Where apprenticeship records exist for the child, the date of the first such event is recorded (some children seem to have been passed from master to master, or masters preferred to pay a fine rather than take a child, a fact which may possibly suggest some physical or mental disability in the child. Stigma could be a factor but does not seem to have prevented other bastard children being placed. The final column in my database is for any other relevant information which has come to light. However it should be noted that some names are so common that it has proved impossible to identify positively which woman of that name is being referred to; these entries are indicated with a question mark (?). (See also the note below about bastard-prone cultures.)

This database has enabled some previously separate sets of data to be identified as relating to one event. A very few entries may actually duplicate an event but there is insufficient evidence to make a link yet. The database is being expanded and added to as more information comes to light.

All consulted writers agree that the incidence of bastardy

increased during the late eighteenth and nineteenth centuries, reaching a peak between 1842 and 1845, before falling as the century progressed; this is contrary to the sentiment expressed by the Ossett incumbent. The period under consideration in this study is, perhaps, too short to enable long-term trends to be evaluated and analysed, but Chart 1 does seem to indicate rates which start to fall much sooner than the national rates, in contrast to the chart derived from figures provided in a broader study in Bastardy and its Comparative History, which shows ratios continuing to rise (Figure 3).

Taking illegitimate births as a percentage of all births gives the bastardy ratio. The significance of this has been questioned since the overall birthrate is itself subject to fluctuations, in that if marital fertility decreases the bastardy ratio will apparently increase even if the number of bastards remains stable. A more reliable measure of the extent of bastardy is the bastardy rate which relates the number of bastards to the number of women of child-bearing age in the population, but the data here is insufficient to enable the calculation of a meaningful figure. Such data is rarely available before c1850.[7]

Working only with the 126 bastards identified from the Census listing, the Bastardy Ratios are

0-5	5-10	10-15	15-20
(1816-1821)	(1811-1816)	(1806-1811)	(1801-1806)
5.88%	6.3%	4.43%	1.96%

It has to be stressed that these figures are based on only those children surviving in these particular age groups and not, as is more usual, on baptismal records, a fact which could account for the decline in the 10-15 and 15-20 age groups, although the even more marked decline in the latter group is presumable influenced by factors already referred to, by the known tendency to migration of young adults, or by the fact that some of that group were apprenticed to masters outside the area of the township. I feel that little faith can be placed in the census data for children over the age of ten; mortality, migration, and apprenticeship have almost certainly reduced the figures to a (statistically) meaningless residue. In *Family Life and Illicit Love in Earlier Generations*, P Laslett quotes, amongst a plethora of bastardy ratios for different times and places, a figure of 3.2 percent for the North during the period 1781-1820.

Was there a bastardy-prone subculture? Of the eighty-three unmarried mothers derived from the census, 58 (69.88%) have one bastard only (singletons); the rest (30.12%) have more than one (repeaters); figures for the country range from 37percent in Devon to

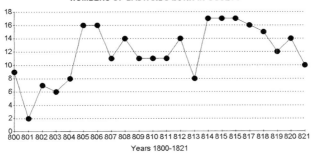

NUMBERS OF BASTARDS BORN IN OSSETT

Years 1800-1821

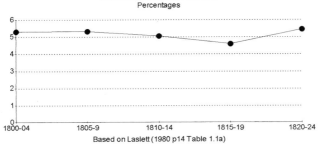

NATIONAL BASTARDY RATIOS
Percentages

Based on Laslett (1980 p14 Table 1.1a)

Figure 3. Charts comparing the incidence of Bastardy in Ossett with national figures.

19 percent in the West Riding with 14.7% in Banbury and 21.8 percent in Hartland.[8] Two women are shown in the census as having five bastards each, but further evidence indicates a maximum, so far, of six. The mean number of children per bastard-bearer, in the census, is 1.51. Taking the whole of the database of 267 events, 28.97 percent of mothers were repeaters, with 52.6 percent of the illegitimate children born to these repeaters. At its simplest the concept of the bastardy-prone sub-culture describes groups, with kinship, social or proximity connections, within which bastardy appears to be significantly more common than in the rest of that society.[9] In this Ossett study one family, the Dews, stand out from the rest; three males father four bastards but there are not less than eleven females involved, who have between them 27 bastards (there are eighty Dews adults listed in the 1821 census – more than 10 percent of the bastards produced by 1.7 percent of the population). Other names appear with some frequency: five Wilby females with nine bastards and three Wilby males with four between them (more than forty Wilbys); five Bold females have nine bastards (four singletons and a repeater with five children) but no Bold males are named as fathers (there are, however, only six Bold females shown in the 1821 census – possible suggesting a bastardy-proneness of staggering proportions!) Out of seventy-nine Ellises, seven females and five males have bastard children. Sixty-five Smiths with four and

three.; thirty Harraps only produce one bastard-bearer; thirty-three Brookes produce six males who beget bastards but no women who bear any. It should perhaps be re-iterated that the population present on the 1821 listing does not necessarily include those involved in procreating bastards but merely serves to illustrate something of the frequency of certain surnames.

Although the 1821 census gives no addresses, the dwellings are listed and numbered and it is probable that houses which are close in the listing are also close in reality, especially where the poorer areas of the town are concerned. If this were so, then it would appear that there are clusters of houses which form such a bastardy-prone sub-culture. Amongst these are the houses numbered 77 and 78 in the listing which form one small cluster, 580, 581, 583 and 584 a larger one, and 914, 916, 918, 920, 926 and 932 another. Nine of the dwellings (not counting the workhouse) contain illegitimate children positively identified as being of more than one mother.

There may be suspicion, but no evidence, of incest: a widower with two daughters still at home who have three bastards between them and only one Bastardy Order for a putative father, is amongst a handful of cases which look questionable. Some of the repeaters name a different man on each occasion; is this evidence of serial monogamy or of prostitution? Given that women were often persuaded to name a father for their child, and that no other evidence was necessary the ability to name the father does not necessarily rule out prostitution.[10]

Between 1800 and 1849 the mean age at first marriage was 25.3 for males and 23.4 for females in England[11]. In the eighty events of bastardy where the age of the mother can be deduced, the mean age for all mothers, including repeaters, is 25.5 with a standard deviation of 6.23; the mean age at the birth of the first bastard, for the forty-four mothers for whom the information is available, is 23.11, with a standard deviation of 5.18, giving an age for the first conception quite close to that of the marriage.

In 172 cases the name of the putative father has been ascertained. 150 different men are so named, with a maximum of four bastards per man. Where the age and occupation of the putative father can be established, they are almost always young, single, working-class men with only a few identified as middle-aged married fathers. 175 females produced the first 267 bastards identified.

It has been suggested that bastards are most likely to be found in households with their mother as a single parent, and in decreasing order of probability in the households of their grandparents with their own parents absent, in households with their parents and legitimate siblings, in institutions, as lodgers, or alone with their fathers.[12] Of 987 inhabited homes in Ossett, seventy-nine (8%) dwellings contain bastards. Of these forty contain three generations and eleven are single-parent families. Thirteen of the households contain no one who could be the mother of the bastard. Of the seventy-nine, nine households contain a married couple and illegitimate children; in one case the child has been identified as being the child of both parents but born before the marriage; although the child is only four years old it has been labelled as illegitimate and given its mother's maiden name. An older child might have become accustomed to its name and resistant to change but this would hardly apply to a four year old. This looks like the work of an over-zealous enumerator/overseer. Several other children have been identified as the child of only one of the parents in the household, usually the mother, but in five households it is quite impossible to make any rational speculation about its composition . In the Ossett workhouse a two-year old male bastard appears to be located with other male inmates and his mother and female sibling accommodated with the other females. It is known that such separate-sex accommodation was provided at Ossett. Only one instance of children being with a solitary male has been identified.

Notes and References

1. Oxley, GW, *Poor relief in England and Wales 1601-1834,* London, 1974, David and Charles, p.74
2. Laslett, P, Oosterveen, K and Smith R M (eds), *Bastardy and its Comparative History,* Cambridge, 1980, Arnold. p 4
3. Burn, R, *The Justice of the Peace and Parish Officer* , London, 1820, Cadell et al.
4. Burn, op cit, p.238
5. *Ibid.*
6. *Ibid.*
7. Laslett, *op.cit.*
8. Laslett, P. *Family Life and Illicit Love in Earlier Generations,* Cambridge, 1977 Cambridge.
9. Laslett, Oosterveen, and Smith R M *op. cit*
10. Webb, S and B, *English Poor Law History, pt 1, pt 2,* Vols. 1 and 2, London, 1963 rpt, Cass and Co. p. 309
11. Tranter, N L, *Population and Society 1750-1940,* London, 1985, Longman. p 52
12. Laslett, Oostervven and Smith, *op.cit*

Additional Bibliography

Mount, F, *The Subversive Family: an alternative history of love and marriage,* London, 1985, Cape.
Tranter, N L, *Population and Society 1750-1940.* London, 1985, Longman.

Primary Sources

1807 Poll Book for the Yorkshire election*
1821 Census enumerators' books for Ossett cum Gawthorpe township*
Militia List*
Poor Law papers, including Bastardy Book*
Ossett Green Congregationalist Chapel, baptismal records**
Ossett Methodist Chapel, baptismal records**
Ossett Chapel of Ease (Dewsbury Parish), baptismal records***
* in the John Goodchild Collection.
** in Wakefield Library HQ, Balne Lane, Wakefield.
*** In West Yorkshire Archives, Newstead Road, Wakefield.

Appendices

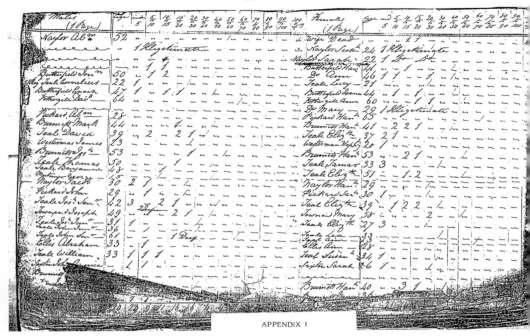

APPENDIX 1

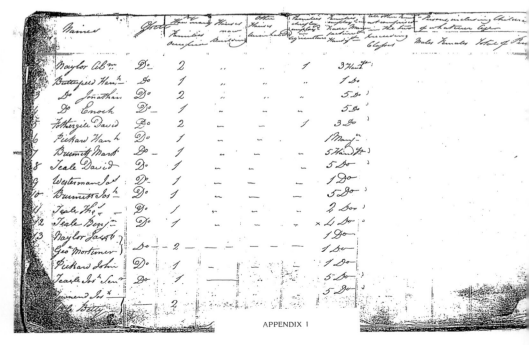

APPENDIX 1

#	Mother	Age	1821	B.Bk	Bap	Child(age)	Father	Age/Occ	App	Comments
1	Audsley, Eliz(Betty)			1812			Kemp, Wm	ML 20/clothier		
2	Audsley, Sarah			1811		(dec)	Ward, Saml			
3	Audsley, Sarah			1813		(dec)	Ward, Saml			
4	Baines, Rachel			1815	1815	Susy*	Hinchcliffe, Joseph	ML 25/clothier		married
5	Batty, Eliz				1821	Mary				
6	Batty, Jane (widow)				1814	John				
7	Beaumont, Eliz			1808			Roberts, Joseph			
8	Beavins?, Ellen				1813	Joseph				
9	Bold, Ann				1810	?M....			1822	
10	Bold, Christiana			1806		(dec)	Crabtree, Wm			
11	Bold, Hannah	15	35	1805	1805	Harriett	Leather, Ri			
12	Bold, Hannah	17	35	1807		?Wm	Shaw, John			15 yr old app Wm in 1821
13	Bold, Hannah	24	35	1810	1810	Mary	Brook, Ri	ML 35/clothier 4ch		
14	Bold, Hannah	16	35		1802	John				
15	Bold, Maria	18	35		1804	Mary				
16	Bold, Maria	20	41	1800			Shotton, Francis			
17	Bold, Sarah				1806	Matilda			1818*	
18	Boocock, Hannah			1805		Harriett(16)	Hitchin, Ro			
19	Braithwaite, Sarah				1816	Wm Mitchel				
20	Brear, Ann			1809		Susanna	Smith, John			
21	Brear, Ann			1811		Margaret	Day, Wm			
22	Brear, Ann			1815		Ann	Day, Wm			RO1811 to Ossett
23	Brear, Ann				1802	James				
24	Britton, Martha	33	55	1803			Scott, Ro			
25	Brogden, Mary	31	36	1816	1816	Joseph	Lockwood, John		1831	
26	Brogden, Mary	26	36		1811	William				
27	Brook, Alice			1819			Robinson, Joseph	ML 29/clothier 5ch		married
28	Brummet, Leah			1805	1805	Seth (dec)	Fothergill, Jos	ML 24/clothier		
29	Burton, Mary			1816		female	Stephenson, John			- married, aet 30 min 1821, clothier
30	Burton, Mary				1814	Sarah				
31	Burton, Nanny			1808		female	Brummett, David			
32	Butterfield, Hannah	24	41		1804	Harriett				
33	Chapel, Eliz			1819	1819	Mary (dec)	Ramsden, Benj			
34	Chapel, Judith			1811	1811	David(9)	Kendal, Judah	ML 21/clothier		married
35	Clark, Eliz	16	35	1802			Wood, Joseph			
36	Clark, Eliz	22	35	1808			Overend, Wm			
37	Clark, Eliz	28	35	1814			Ellis, David	ML 3l/clothier 4ch		
38	Clark, Mary			1816		(dec)	Westerman, Thos			

#	Mother	Age	1821	B.Bk	Bap	Child(age)	Father	Age/Occ	App	Comments
39	Clegg, Eliz(Betty)			1820	1820	Ruth	Cookson, Hy			
40	Clegg, Hannah			1814			Carter, Jos			
41	Clegg, Hannah			1817	1817	Thos	Garforth, Jacob			married
42	Clegg, Maria	34	47	1808	1808	John	Marsden, Wm	ML 26/clothier		married
43	Conyer, Eliz(Betty)	32	33		1820	Geo				
44	Crowther, Hannah		35							
45	Curtis, Ann				1820	Ann				
46	Curtis, Eliz		26							
47	Dews, Ann	28	44	1805	1805	?Lillian	Ellis, Titus			
48	Dews, Ann	39	44	1816	1815	Ann	Hemingway, Ri			
49	Dews, Ann	23	44	1800		Martha	Morehouse, Wm			
50	Dews, Ann	35	44		1812	Mary Martha				
51	Dews, Ann	40	44		1817	Charlotte				
52	Dews, Ann	41	44		1818	Jane				
53	Dews, Eliz(Betty)			1808	1807	Sarah	Chapel, John			
54	Dews, Hannah	21	30	1812			Burton, wm	ML 21/clothier		
55	Dews, Hannah	26	30	1817			Burton, Wm	ML 21/clothier		
56	Dews, Maria			1807			Phillip, Thos	PB gent		
57	Dews, Martha	27	39	1809	1809	Eliz	Ellis, Wm			
58	Dews, Martha	22	39	1804			Wilby, Jeremiah			
59	Dews, Martha (pauper)	32	39	1814	1814	George	Wilby, Jeremiah			
60	Dews, Mary	?15	?24	1812			Hanson, James			
61	Dews, Mary	21	24	1818	1818	Judith	Ainsley(aka Lister),Geo			
62	Dews, Sarah	20	26	1815			Teal, David			
63	Dews, Sarah	25	26		1820	Rachel				
64	Dews, Susan		?l	1816			Hemingway, Ri			
65	Dews, Susan		?l	1817			Pollard, Joseph	ML 22/clothier		
66	Dews, Susannah		?l	1806			Calverley, Jos			
67	Dews, Susannah		?l	1811	1811	Eliz	Hindle, Jeremiah			
68	Dews, Susannah		?l		1802	Mary				
69	Dews, Susannah		?l		1809	Mary Ann				
70	Dews, Susannah		?l		1814	Mary Ann				
71	Dews, Susannah		?l		1821	Sarah				
72	Dews, Susannah,jun		?l	1816	1816	Nathan	Kitson, Joseph			
73	Dews, Sussey		?l							RO 1820 to Ossett
74	Eastwood, Hannah			1817	1817	Wm	Stead, John			
75	Eastwood, Martha	36	43	1814	1814	Charlotte	Speight, Adam			
76	Ellis, Ann		?l	1806		female	Illingworth, Wm			

#	Mother	Age	1821	B.Bk	Bap	Child(age)	Father	Age/Occ	App	Comments
77	Ellis, Ann		?l		1814	George				
78	Ellis, Eliz		?l		1805	John				
79	Ellis, Mary		?l	1812	1812	Joseph W	Whitaker, Wm			
80	Ellis, Nancy			1804			Kilburn, Joseph			
81	Ellis, Rachel	21	26	1816			Bradley, Geo			
82	Ellis, Sarah		?l		1812	Nancy				
83	Elsworth, Eliz		26							
84	Emerson, Hannah				1810	Eliza	Hartley, Saml			
85	Emley, Sarah			1814			Fligg, Joseph			
86	Emley, Sarah			1819	1819	Eliza	Fligg, Joseph			
87	Fearnley, Mary			1817	1817	Joseph	Liley, Joshua		1831	
88	Fletcher, Ann		35			male child				
89	Fletcher, Ann		35			male child				
90	Fletcher, Ann		35			male child				
91	Fothergill, Eliz			1818	1818	Emma(dec)	Teal, John	ML 24/clothier		
92	Fothergill, Mary	24	29	1816			Watson, John			
93	Fozard, Mary			1815			Nowell, James			
94	Furniss, Lydia			1805			Dews, Jno			
95	G(J)agger, Betty			1815	1815	Geo	Lodge, John			
96	G(J)agger, Susannah				1817	Jeremiah				
97	Gibson, Sarah			1804			Naylor, Ro			
98	Giggle, Jemima	24	33	1812	1812	Robert	Butterfield, Mark			
99	Giggle, Martha	24	34	1811			Driver, Thos			
100	Giggle, Martha	30	34	1817	1817		Whitaker, J (dec)	ML 42/clothier		
101	Giggle, Martha	31	34	1818			Gouldon, Jno			
102	Giggle, Martha	28	34		1815	Ellen				
103	Giggle, Martha	28	34		1815	Mary				
104	Glover, Hannah				1800	James				
105	Glover, Mary			1815			Archer, Jesse			
106	Goldthorpe, Mary	19	25	1815	1815	Francis	Mitchel, Geo	ML 19/clothier		
107	Gomersal, Eliz(Betty)		n/s	1812			Crossland, John			
108	Gomersal, Sarah			1804	1804	Martha(17)	Stubley, Joseph		1813+	
109	Gomersal, Sarah				1810	Martha				
110	Gomersal, Sarah				1812	Hannah(12)				
111	Haigh, Fanny			1819	1819	Wm	Charlesworth, Mi			
112	Haigh, Sarah				1817	Geo				
113	Hall, Rachel				1803	Mary				
114	Hampshire, Mary	19	20		1821	Chas				

	Mother	Age	1821	B.Bk	Bap	Child(age)	Father	Age/Occ	App	Comments
115	Hanson, Eliz			1809		male	Brooke, Joseph	ML 18/clothier		
116	Hanson, Mary			1818	1818	Jane(dec)	Miller, Joseph			
117	Hargrave, Eliz		42	1806			Hirst, Thos			
118	Hargrave, Eliz		42	1809		?Martin	Graham, Martin		?1815	
119	Harrap, Patience	19	23	1817	1817	Fanny	Crowther, Saml			
120	Harrap, Patience	21	23	1819	1819	John	Westerman, Jas			
121	Heald, Frances			1798			Burton, James			
122	Heald, Frances				1808	Wm	Giggal, Benj			
123	Heald, Frances				1810	James				
124	Heald, Hannah	28	?44	1805			Smith, Frank	ML 22/clothier		married
125	Heald, Hannah	23	?44		1800	Nathan	Sharp, John		1813	
126	Hebdin, Hannah			1810		Sarah	Whitaker, Wm			aet 23/1809
127	Hebdin, Hannah			1814			Lawrence, Wm			married
128	Hemingway, Alice				1815	Charles				RO 1815to Stanley
129	Hemingway, Betty	32	45	1808	1808	Thos	Oldroyd, John		1822	
130	Henley, Sarah		27			female				
131	Hepper, Alice	21	22		1821	Thos				
132	Hepworth, Ann				1806	Mary				
133	Hinchcliffe, Sarah	17	29	1809	1809	Thomas	Ward, David	ML 21/clothier		
134	Hopkin, Mary			1810			Arnald, Wm			
135	Hopton, Amelia			1805		?Thos	Illingworth, Jos	ML 35/clothier	1815	
136	Huntington, Sarah				1808	Eliz				RO1808
137	Ibbotson, Hannah	20	26	1815	1815	John	Mitchel, Joshua	PB clothier		married
138	Ibbotson, Judith	17	17		1821	Mary				
139	Jackson, ?		8			Wm				
140	Kemp, Rachel	21	28	1814			Horsfall, Ri			
141	Kemp, Rachel	25	28	1818			Horsfall, Ri			
142	Kemp, Sarah		33			male				
143	Kendal, Nancy	21	24	1818			Godley, John			
144	Lambert, Rhoda				1801					
145	Land, Eve	21	37	1805			Audsley, Joseph	ML 25/cordwnr lch		
146	Land, Eve	24	37	1808			Audsley, Joseph	ML 25/cordwnr lch		
147	Land, Eve	28	37	1812			Audsley, Joseph	ML 25/cordwnr lch		
148	Land, Eve	34	37	1818			Fligg, Joseph			
149	Land, Hannah		?!	1818	1818	Mary	North, Ri			
150	Land, Sarah			1810			Marsden, Wm	ML 26/clothier		
151	Land, Sarah				1820	Martha				
152	Lee, Ann		20			female				

	Mother	Age	1821	B.Bk	Bap	Child(age)	Father	Age/Occ	App	Comments
153	Lee, Mary			1811			Westerby, John			
154	Lockwood, Hannah		?	1813			Fligg, Jos		nd	
155	Longley, Hannah			1809	1809	Jno	Exley, John			
156	Lucas, Hannah	20	34	1807			Ellis, David	ML 31/clothier 4ch		
157	Marsden, Martha				1816	Hannah				
158	Marsden, Martha				1818	Mary				
159	Marsden, Martha				1819	Benj				
160	Marsden, Martha				1821	Frank				
161	Mawson, Betty			1807			Riley, Joseph			
162	Mawson, Betty			1815			Townend, Joseph			
163	Mitchell, Mary				1813	Thomas	Crook, John			
164	Mitchell, Sarah	27	39	1809	1809	Mary	Hall, Thos	ML 40/chapman		
165	Mitchell, Sarah	28	39	1810			Fligg, Nathaniel	ML 23/clothier		
166	Mitchell, Sarah	39	39		1821	Joseph				
167	Moorby, Ann			1804		(dec)	Wood, T (dec)			
168	Moorhouse, Eliz(dec)			1798			Senior, Thos			
169	Moorhouse, Eliz(dec)			1805	1805	Hannah	Lodge, Jacob			
170	Moorhouse, Eliz(dec)			1815			Johnson, Wm			
171	Moorhouse, Eliz(dec)			1818		male	Boocock, Ri			
172	Moorhouse, Eliz(dec)					female				
173	Moorhouse, Susannah			1805	1805	Mary	Carver, Geo			
174	Morris, Eliz			1813			Fox, Eli			
175	Moss, Hannah	32	36		1817	Eliza				
176	Moss, Hannah	36	36		1821	Ann				
177	Moss, Mary		32	1817			Whitaker, Wm			
178	Moss, Mary		32	1817			Whitaker, Wm			
179	Moss, Mary		32		1815	Jane				
180	Moss, Susannah	25	45		1805	Mary				
181	Musgrave, Mary			1813	1813	Sarah	White, John			
182	Musgrave, Sarah				1813	Sarah				
183	Naylor, Martha				1820	Martha				
184	Naylor, Sarah		22			female				
185	Naylor, Susey	19	24	1816			Wilby, Thos	ML 24/clothier		
186	Newton, Martha			1801			Nowele, Geo			
187	Oldroyd, Eliz			1816			Gaunt, Saml			
188	Oldroyd, Mary		24							
189	Oxley, Hannah			1816	1816	Wm	Cooper, John			
190	Parkinson, Ann		35?	1800			Senior, Jno			

	Mother	Age	1821	B.Bk	Bap	Child(age)	Father	Age/Occ	App	Comments
191	Parkinson, Ann		35?	1800			Harrop, Senior			
192	Peace, Mary			1806			Lucas, Joseph			married
193	Pickersgill, Hannah			1800	1800	David	Preston, Wm		1813	
194	Pickersgill, Rachel				1821	Sarah				
195	Pollard,Eliz				1812	Harriett				
196	Radley, Ann			1804		Mary	Illingworth, Thos	ML 26/clothier		
197	Radley, Ann			1807			Illingworth, Thos	ML 26/clothier		
198	Radley, Mary				1807	Geo				
199	Radley, Sarah			1809	1809	John	Saxton, Abr'm	ML 24/clothier		married
200	Raikes, Hannah			1803			Spurr, John			
201	Rayner, Ann				1808	Nathan				
202	Rayner, Hannah		35							
203	Rayner, Mary Ann			1805		(dec)	Marsden, Jos	ML 27/clothier lch		
204	Rayner, Mary Ann			1806		Jos (16)	Marsden, Jos	ML27/clothier lch		
205	Redfearn, Hannah			1803			Siswick, Joseph			
206	Redfearn, Hannah			1809	1808	Susanna	Bates, John			
207	Riley, Ann			1805			Brooke, Benj			
208	Robinson, Fanny			1818	1818	Jas P dec	Pickersgill, Benj	ML 18.clothier		
209	Robinson, Maria		33			male				
210	Robinson, Maria		33			male				
211	Robinson, Mary			1816	1816	Wm	Evens, Jabez			
212	Robinson, Mary			1819	1819	John	Evens, Jabez			RO 1819
213	Ruddlesden, Esther	26	33	1814			Haigh, Job			
214	Ruddlesden, Rebecca		31			female				
215	Scott, Rachel			1806	1804	Jane	Hinchcliffe, J	ML 25/clothier		
216	Seed, Ann			1803		(dec)	Sharp, Joseph			
217	Senior, Martha	24	25		1820	Robert				
218	Senior, Sarah			1814			Graham, James			
219	Sheard, Eliz		38			male				
220	Shephard, Charlotte			1812			Beaumont, Thos			
221	Smith, Hannah			1807	1807	Mark	Poole, Wm			
222	Smith, Isabella	21	25	1817	1817	Ann	Ellis, James			married
223	Smith, Sarah		?!	1808	1808	Eliz	Dews, Thos	ML 20/clothier		
224	Smith, Sarah		18		1820	Ann				
225	Speight, Eliz	27	28	1820			Wainwright, Francis			
226	Spence, Nanny			1815			Bains, Joseph			RO1814
227	Teal, Hannah				1800					
228	Teal, Susanna				1810		Hall, Wm			

	Mother	Age	1821	B.Bk	Bap	Child(age)	Father	Age/Occ	App	Comments
229	Tolson, Amelia	20	22	1819		male	Spurr, Joseph			
230	Vicars, Ann			1802		James(18)	Smith, Thos			
231	Wade, Mary				1818	Jane				
232	Wade, Mary				1814	Thomas(6)				
233	Ward, Ann	21	37	1805		female	Scott, Saml	PB clothier		
234	Ward, Ann	27	37	1811		male	Scott, Saml	PB clothier		
235	Ward, Ann	31	37	1815		male	Clegg, Nathaniel	ML 27/labourer lch		
236	Ward, Mary	?14	21		1814	Jane				
237	Westerman, Hannah	29	34	1816			Wilson, Geo			
238	Westerman, Lydia			1800		Geo				
239	Westerman, Sarah					Joseph	Saxton, John			
240	White, Sarah	24	42	1803			Hill, Ro			
241	White, Sarah	26	42	1805			Marsden, Francis			
242	White, Sarah	32	42	1811	1811	?Enoch			1824	
243	White, Sarah	21	42		1802	John	Hill, Ro			
244	Wilby, Ann			1808			Pickersgill, Joseph			
245	Wilby, Ann			1809		female	Shaw, Joseph			
246	Wilby, Ann									RO1815 to Glasshoughton pregnant
247	Wilby, Christiana			1806	1806	Hannah	Dews, John			
248	Wilby, Christiana			1812		James(9)	Dews, John			
249	Wilby, Hannah				1802	Mark			1814	
250	Wilby, Rhoda	28	32	1817	1818	Emma	Burton, Geo			
251	Wilby, Sarah	19	23	1817	1817	Joshua	Heald, Isaac			
252	Wilby, Sarah	21	23		1819	Wm				
253	Wilby, Sarah	22	23		1820	Charles				
254	Wild, Eliz	31	?33	1819			Chapel, Thos			
255	Wild, Eliz	26	?33		1814	Sarah				
256	Wild, Eliz	32	?33		1820	Jane				
257	Wild, Grace (pauper)			1818	1818	Sarah	Wrigley, Benj			
258	Wilkinson, Hannah		30			female				
259	Wilson, Martha			1807	1807	Ann	Gower, Edward			
260	Wilson, Mary			1800	1800	Sarah	Wilby, Isaac	ML35/clothier 3ch		
261	Wilson, Sarah			1816			Brook, Mark			
262	Wilson, Sarah				1820	Martha				
263	Wood, Ann			1807		(dec)	Brooke, Thos	ML 31/joiner lch		
264	Wood, Ann			1811			Brooke, Thos	ML 31/joiner lch		
265	Wright, ?		6			Geo				
266	Wright, Hannah				1808	Wm				
267	Wroe, Martha				1808	James				
268										

KEY TO APPENDIX 2
=================================

Column No	Field Name	Comments/Explanation
1	Mother	Name of mother
2	Age	Approximate age of mother at birth of that particular child
3	1821	Age of mother as given in 1821 census listing
4	B Bk	Date of Bastardy Order
5	Bap	Date of baptism of child
6	Child(age)	Name or gender of child, with, in brackets, age as given in 1821 census
7	Father	Name of putative father
8	Age/Occ	Source of information and father's age, occupation and number of children ML = Militia List PB = 1807 Poll Book
9	App	Date of child's first (or only) apprenticeship
10	Comments	Any other relevant information (RO = Removal Order and its date)

9. A 200 YEAR LEGACY OF THE 1793 WAKEFIELD INCLOSURE

by John Goodchild, M Univ

IN MARCH 1876 SIR EDMUND BECKETT, Queen's Counsel, rose in a House of Lords committee to inform their lordships that he had to tell them what he described as 'a most extraordinary story, a story of a kind perfectly unique in my long experience here' – and he had been a barrister for some 35 years. (Figure 1) The unique story which he was to tell them was a Wakefield story, and he got it wrong; only with the recent discovery of documents relating to the story has its detail become more clear. Although Sir Edmund Beckett was employed in 1876 to bring that story to an end, in fact he and the others involved at that time were unsuccessful, and the story continued until 1972.

What the story was about was certainly curious. When in 1793 Parliament passed an act to inclose and to divide into private fields what had hitherto been the open commons, village greens, strip fields and water meadows of Wakefield, Alverthorpe cum Thornes, and Stanley cum Wrenthorpe townships, that was the first such inclosure of any township within his manor made with the full approval of the Duke of Leeds, lord of the great Manor of Wakefield which stretched from Normanton in the east up to the Lancashire boundary in the west. Under the commons, which included the 2,500-acre Wakefield Outwood as well as the lesser Eastmoor, Thornes Moor, Westgate

Figure 1. Transcript of Sir. Edmund Becke speech of 22 March 1876 raising the 'uniq story of the liability imposed on those v acquired land under the 1793 Wakefi Inclosure Act. *The John Goodchild Collection.*

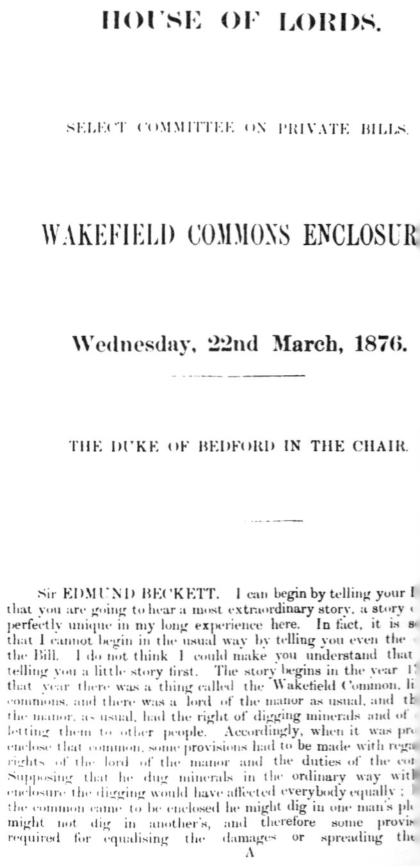

HOUSE OF LORDS.

SELECT COMMITTEE ON PRIVATE BILLS.

WAKEFIELD COMMONS ENCLOSUR

Wednesday, 22nd March, 1876.

THE DUKE OF BEDFORD IN THE CHAIR.

Sir EDMUND BECKETT. I can begin by telling your I that you are going to hear a most extraordinary story, a story perfectly unique in my long experience here. In fact, it is so that I cannot begin in the usual way by telling you even the the Bill. I do not think I could make you understand that telling you a little story first. The story begins in the year 1 that year there was a thing called the Wakefield Common, li commons, and there was a lord of the manor as usual, and the the manor, as usual, had the right of digging minerals and of letting them to other people. Accordingly, when it was pro enclose that common, some provisions had to be made with rega rights of the lord of the manor and the duties of the co Supposing that he dug minerals in the ordinary way wit enclosure the digging would have affected everybody equally ; the common came to be enclosed he might dig in one man's pl might not dig in another's, and therefore some provis required for equalising the damages or spreading the

A

Moor, Whinney Moor and various other pieces of village green and common, the coal was reserved, as was usual in such inclosures by act of Parliament, to the lord of the manor; he also received the usual one sixteenth of the surface land. But the *Wakefield Inclosure Act* contained an almost unique provision, presumably introduced at the behest of the barrister who was then Steward of the Manor, or even possibly by Robert Lumb, the Wakefield attorney who was Deputy Steward (Figure 2.). This provided that not only were the coal – and other minerals too, though they were less significant – reserved as usual to the Duke of Leeds as lord of the manor, but power was given for this coal to be worked by surface works – shafts, railways and so forth – on any of the new allottees' lands (although not to destroy any buildings); the resulting damages were to be not the financial responsibility of the lord or of his coalmining lessees but that of the whole of the allottees and their descendants in title. Liability for subsidence of the surface was included. Each year a meeting of the allottees was to be held, who were to appoint a salaried officer (who in fact was to work on a part-time basis) who would arrange for the laying, levying upon the whole of the allottees, and distribution of the proceeds of a rate, sometimes annually and more frequently at longer intervals. The present writer's father, the owner of a house built in the 1930s in Thornes Road in Wakefield but upon the site of Thornes Moor, received notices of his assessment from time to time, and grumblingly paid them. Notice of the annual meetings of the allottees appeared in the columns of the *Wakefield Express*, often with a report later of the meeting itself.

This then was the origin of the curious situation where damages caused by coalmining were the financial responsibility not of those who caused them but of those who, collectively, suffered from them. The situation was to continue long after the coming into operation of the nationalisation of coal resources under the act of 1938 and of the coal industry in 1947. This was a situation unique to Wakefield and its out-townships, except for Horbury where the *Inclosure Act of 1809* repeated the provisions but no documentary evidence has been forthcoming as to their having been implemented there, and certainly not into modern times as in Wakefield and its immediate vicinity.

The actual division of the commons, wastes and greens into fields under the *Wakefield Inclosure Act 1793* occurred from 1793 to 1796 and the allottees had their allotment forms – their title deed to their new properties – by 1796. Although coal had been worked, especially in the Outwood, since medieval times, and under Westgate Common from 1791, it was apparently not until 1797 that the first case of compensation for surface damage occurred. This concerned Westgate Common and the fencing of an access road to a colliery, a road which had been built across the allotment awarded at the inclosure to James Burton and used subsequently as pasture and tenter ground. Two arbitrators were appointed, George Leather of Outwood, the agent and engineer to William Fenton, and Jeremiah Clay, but legal counsel considered that fencing costs were the responsibility of the coal owner, the Duke of Leeds, and the case was probably dropped. But in 1796 the 130 acres on the Outwood near the grandstand, awarded to the vicar of Wakefield, Dr Bacon, in lieu of his small tithes, were let to William Fenton, the great coalmaster – the Coal King of Yorkshire – who was continuing his own and his family's longtime interest in mining coal under the Outwood. It is at least likely that it was the surface damages which the Fenton workings occasioned which led to the first successful claims and the first laying of a rate upon the occupiers of all properties upon the erstwhile commons. Certainly such rates were laid in each year between 1798 and 1805 inclusive, William Fenton being himself a substantial payer of the rate as occupier of the vicar of Wakefield's (surface) land too. Thomas Lake was the officer appointed by the annual meetings of the allottees to assess the damages, and make, lay upon the allottees, and collect a compensation rate; allottees upon the Thornes Moor, for example, paid with all others for damages upon the Outwood. Thomas Lake lived at Newton Lane End, in the (modern and later) village of Outwood; he had been the surveyor appointed by the Wakefield Inclosure Commissioners to oversee and certify the making of the many new roads which gave access to the new fields laid out at inclosure, and in 1809 he was appointed official gamekeeper for the Duke of Leeds within Wakefield and Sandal. He was a farmer at Outwood. He fell from his horse at the end of 1827 and broke his thigh, was treated by Caleb Crowther M D of Wakefield but died. His widow brought a claim for damages against the doctor in the Wakefield Court Baron. Lake was the officer who sent out the claim notes 'for damage done by' the working of the collieries below the surface.

The Fenton colliery ceased working in 1806. However, before working ceased, Captain George Waugh of Wakefield made a claim for damages done to his property of a substantial £264 13s 6d, a claim subsequently renewed and increased to £392 5s. For a time nothing was done, but then the allottees met and appointed a new officer, William Shaw of Southgate in Wakefield, whose main work was as a collector of taxes. The matter of George Waugh's compensation was referred, as the Inclosure Act of 1793 provided, to arbitrators, the aforementioned George Leather and William Dawson, colliery manager, of Wragby, Nostell. They were unable to agree and the matter was left to the decision of William Porter of Garforth, another colliery manager and consultant, who awarded Captain Waugh £364 11s 5d in compensation, to be paid at the *White Hart Inn* in Wakefield, on 13 May 1809. Now this substantial sum was to be laid as a rate, on the basis of the poor-rate valuation – and there was a great deal of commotion about it. In September 1809 twenty-three allottees met at the *Wheel Inn* at Bragg Lane End on the Wakefield to Bradford road at Wrenthorpe and decided to appeal, as they had a right to do under the 1793 Act, to the West Riding Quarter Sessions against the rate, on the basis that (1) Waugh's claim was out of time in its having been made, (2) the officer's power to raise the sum for Waugh's compensation was contested and (3) the rate was inequitable. The allottees entered into an 'Association Agreement' to cover the legal costs involved. These were to be considerable: the lawyer's account for going to London on the matter survives. At the end of 1809 a meeting of allottees was held at which John Maude, of Moor House, Stanley, tried to explain the legal reasons which would prevent an expensive lawsuit. He was heard throughout, at what was apparently a heated meeting, and then told plainly that his reasons were irrelevant. The case had already been before the Quarter Sessions and there adjourned to a later meeting which was held in January 1810, there being a legal question as to the admissability of a mere printed copy of the private Act of 1793, which was not certified as having been compared with the official engrossment of the Act among the records of Parliament: this had to be done. The magistrates decided to remove the case into a higher court and it was sent for decision by the judges in the Court of King's Bench. One of the causes of the rumpus was that the rate was to be laid at ten shillings in the pound and that the valuations of property in the two out-townships of Alverthorpe cum Thornes and Stanley cum Wrenthorpe differed markedly, the former being much lower. In the Court of King's Bench the whole matter was settled in favour of the rate. George Waugh called a meeting of allottees in February 1810. Numbers of these meetings were held in the Moot Hall, the manorial court house in Wakefield.

The matter of the rate arose once more as a dispute about 1820. William Shaw was still officer for the rate and the matter in question concerned the right of William Fenton to lay a railway across the

Outwood to carry his coals to the River Calder and the boats there. The matter ended in High Court action, with Fenton the victor. A rate was collected in 1820 but no meeting of allottees was held in 1821 owing to the court action and by 1824 claims totalled nearly £1,400. Shaw refused to compel payment of the rate unless he was indemnified against legal actions, and in 1825 and 1826 further legal agreements were made to indemnify Shaw and (among the allottees) to pay the expenses of recovering the sums due from individual rate assessments. A committee of four was set up to organise matters, headed by Reverend Samuel Sharp, vicar of Wakefield 1810-1855 and, of course, a major allottee. However there was some dissatisfaction with Shaw as officer, and in 1830 the allottees again met in the Moot Hall, under vicar Sharp's chairmanship, when a Mr Towlerton, who had briefly replaced Shaw, was himself replaced by Joseph Duckworth the younger as

> the officer for settling and ascertaining the Satisfaction to be made for Damages done by the Working of the Collieries of the Duke of Leeds

and for collecting the assessments upon the allottees, at £30 a year to be paid out of the monies he received from the rate. Duckworth had been appointed agent to the Wakefield Gas Company in 1929 and continued as such; he was described in the trade directory of 1837 as share broker, agent and accountant, of Warrengate in Wakefield. He died in March 1841.

There seems now to have been a long period during which the provisions of the *Wakefield Inclosure Act* of 1793 fell into disuse. When in 1874 a new officer was appointed to deal with a new claim, the only previous occasion then known was that of 1825 – nothing before and nothing after. But in 1873 the sinking of Lofthouse Colliery was begun and damages were caused to land on the Outwood belonging to the Governors of Wakefield Grammar School. The Clerk to the Governors, William Walker, a barrister, called a meeting of allottees late in 1874 by newspaper advertisement. Only fourteen allottees attended and the claim for compensation was for only £35, but Walker, the Governors' Clerk was appointed officer by that meeting at £100 a year. Another meeting was then called to inquire what was going on, and although after a year as officer Walker was not reappointed, his own Governors decided that another officer was needed and obtained a High Court order to that effect. In 1876 John Farrer of Oulton, land agent, surveyor and valuer, in practice for 30 years previously, a Fellow of the Institute of Surveyors and a member of the Northern Land Agents' Association, was appointed as the

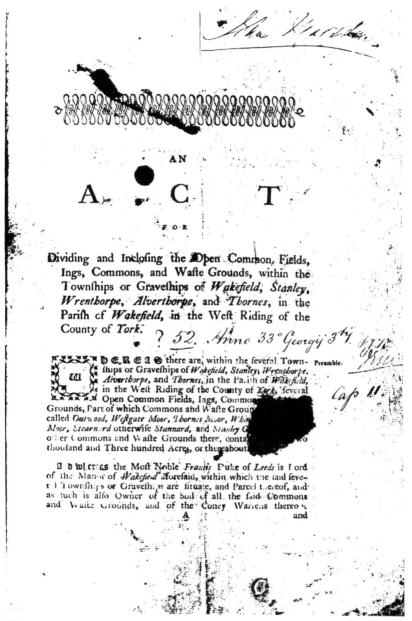

Figure 2. The front page of the *Wakefield Inclosure Act* of 1793.

officer, part time of course. His descendants in that practice held office for about a century.

In 1891 there were 605 allottees – there had been 400 or 500 in the 1790s – and compensation had been made from 1877 to 1890 averaging £90 17s a year while the cost of assessing damages, settling claims, laying rates and legal costs in their recovery etc, averaged £125 a year. Farrer thought that the land liable for this special rate did

> not have a fair chance of being developed. There is yet in the minds of the people of the District a suspicion that unnecessary burthens attach to the lands.

Early in Farrer's period as officer, a scheme was got up to rid the area of this nuisance. The law now provided compensation, although not without the threat of costs to the lord of the manor's estate coal, which the 1793 Act's provisions largely avoided. John Marsden, an elderly but very experienced and able lawyer, was appointed to deal with what was necessary – a new act of Parliament to repeal the old one. Charles Clay, the Wakefield agricultural implement manufacturer, who was a near neighbour of Marsden at Walton, was a leading light in the promotion of the new Bill in Parliament in 1876, with the great Sir Edmund Beckett to support the cause in the House of Lords' Committee. But the Lords' Committee found that the reasons given for the Bill were not proven, although they refused to allow costs to the Governors of the Grammar School who had vehemently opposed it.

The Parliamentary Bill of 1876 having failed, the matter was still strongly felt about locally. Some 100 persons had attended the allottees' meeting in October 1875 before the unsuccessful promotion of the Bill. Farrer continued as the officer, and the size of the financial problem was somewhat alleviated under an agreement made in 1889 whereby the Lofthouse Colliery Company agreed to make an annual payment of £40. In 1891 Charles Clay, still the leading light in opposition to the whole system under the 1793 Act, and the owner of the Stennard Island at Wakefield, one of the commons and on which his works were built, agreed to go with Farrer to London in regard to the current enquiries of the Royal Commission on Mining Royalties, and to seek the promotion of another Act to abolish the 1793 Act's provisions in regard to coal-working compensation. Some three years later a Bill was promoted to buy out the lord of the manor's rights to get minerals without making compensation for surface damages, the compensation money to be raised by means of a final rate and the allottees agreeing to pay John Farrer the cost of promoting the Bill itself. But still nothing occurred in the way of ending the matter and rates for compensation and to cover the officer's costs continued to be laid and paid as need arose – in 1892, 1897, 1901, 1905, 1912, etc. The sums involved now varied enormously. To an extent they had always done so, but now more land was being divided up for house-building plots: in 1906 individual sums due varied between threepence halfpenny and £6 8s 4d. In 1904 a Counsel's opinion suggested that the rate must be laid yearly, as the 1793 Act provided, and the officer was appointed for one year only: no meeting, no officer; he suggested also that the rates laid in 1897 and 1901 were in fact illegally laid. In 1913 a further rate was laid and, as usual, many of the rate demands had been met in the month after the demand was received.

By 1947 there were some 2,000 allottees and the usual payments, made year after year, were to the NCB and to British Rail. Payments were also made to market gardeners affected by coal working, and for land affected by the encroaching Lofthouse spoil heaps, and £100 a year was paid to the officer, J T Dickson, who had held office for two years. Lofthouse Colliery now contributed £70 a year and some £100 a year came from the rate laid. In 1953 a long account appeared in the *Wakefield Express* of one of the annual meetings of the allottees. At this meeting the at least 60 year old system of having a trustees' committee and a chairman was got rid of – they were not provided for in the 1793 Act which envisaged an annual allottees' meeting and the work of a salaried officer. It was stated that some time previously it had been calculated that the cost of an amending Act of Parliament would be £2,000, and an attempt to introduce a repealing clause in a *Wakefield Corporation Act* had been unsuccessful as the area covered by the 1793 Act came in part under the Stanley Urban District Council. Frank Higgins, the Wakefield solicitor, was at this meeting appointed the officer, at a much reduced remuneration of £20 a year, and he proposed to kill the matter by doing nothing at all. He claimed that the Inclosure Act 'would be defunct straight away'. But that was not to be.

Sources

The information in this essay is entirely derived from the Wakefield Inclosure mss in the John Goodchild Collection, Wakefield.

10. ACCURATE RESEARCH CONFOUNDS THE ESTABLISHMENT FOR THE BENEFIT OF THE PUBLIC

by Ronald Swinden

ON 15 SEPTEMBER 1967, as a recently married young man, I received a surprise demand for payment of a rate amounting to thirteen shillings (65p) levied for damages done by working the mines of the Lord of the Manor. This rate demand quoted the *Wakefield Inclosure Act 1793* and had been levied by a land agent surveyor at Oulton, near Leeds, but there was no address or telephone number via which the imposition might be questioned. (Figure 1)

As a legal executive and former search clerk at a Wakefield solicitors', and a former deeds inspector at the West Riding Registry of Deeds, I was trained to be 100% accurate at all times, but I had had no experience of dealing with Inclosure matters. I did know, however, that a demand such as I had received relative to the joint ownership of our recently-purchased property at Kirkhamgate was an incumbrance which should have been disclosed to my solicitors and ourselves when the purchase was being completed.

Accordingly I examined my deeds and found no confirmation. I also traced the sender of the demand and was politely informed that such demands had been levied for over 100 years and that the sum would have to be paid. I was also told that such rate demands had been challenged many times by solicitors and barristers, some of whom had

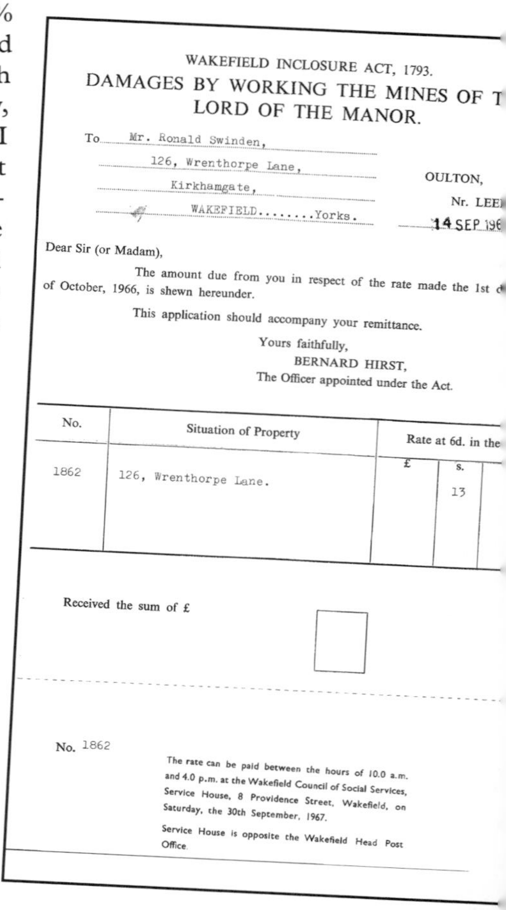

WAKEFIELD INCLOSURE ACT, 1793.

DAMAGES BY WORKING THE MINES OF T[HE] LORD OF THE MANOR.

To   Mr. Ronald Swinden,

126, Wrenthorpe Lane,

Kirkhamgate,

WAKEFIELD.......Yorks.

OULTON,

Nr. LEE[DS]

14 SEP 196[7]

Dear Sir (or Madam),

The amount due from you in respect of the rate made the 1st d[ay] of October, 1966, is shewn hereunder.

This application should accompany your remittance.

Yours faithfully,

BERNARD HIRST,

The Officer appointed under the Act.

No.	Situation of Property	Rate at 6d. in the [£]	
		£	s.
1862	126, Wrenthorpe Lane.		13

Received the sum of £

No. 1862

The rate can be paid between the hours of 10.0 a.m. and 4.0 p.m. at the Wakefield Council of Social Services, Service House, 8 Providence Street, Wakefield, on Saturday, the 30th September, 1967.

Service House is opposite the Wakefield Head Post Office.

Figure 1. The rate demand which alerted the author to the problem of liability for damages incurred during mine-working. *Courtesy of Ronald Swinden.*

been instructed by the courts that they were perfectly legal.

Some 3,000 similar demands had been sent to others over a wide area from Bottomboat to Kirkhamgate, Lupset, Thornes and Sandal, but there had been an unusual number of complaints so a meeting was to be held at which matters would be explained. This took place on 14 October 1967, with 21 people attending, mostly in angry mood. The officer appointed under the Inclosure Act gave an explanation, but soon an adjournment was approved to allow the members of Parliament for Wakefield and Normanton to be present together with the Town Clerk of Wakefield and the Clerk of Stanley U D C, in order that they might give advice as to how the Act might be repealed or certain clauses be deleted.

Inclosure Acts provided for the sharing out of common land amongst those who had previously had rights relating to it. Further research revealed that the *Wakefield Inclosure Act 1793* was almost unique as it included a clause indicating that when the Lord of the Manor received access to all the minerals (mainly coal and fireclay) beneath the surface of the commons being allotted to those who qualified, and he wished to exploit them, he would be absolved from any claim for damage. This was, in effect, an insurance clause: it provided that if he or his colliery agents exercised his right to enter any land, those who suffered damages should claim from those who did not suffer; an officer was appointed to administer the claims and make payments, deducting a salary for his work. Owners of property allotted under the inclosure paid a rate to provide the funds from which compensation could be paid. This procedure had been followed from 1873 onwards, or earlier, as shafts were sunk or a reservoir or railway made on, or over, land which had been allotted. Obviously since then there had been two world wars and other significant events.

At the resumed hearing, when 84 people were present, I learned of those making claims; they included the National Coal Board, British Rail, and four private individuals. Not suprisingly I made the most telling legal challenges and was forthwith appointed chairman of an ad hoc committee, which included the deputy Town Clerk of Wakefield at my suggestion, charged with investigating the claims that had given rise to the levying of the rate. All claimants were requested to prove their claims to me. I was able to rebut the N C B claim on the grounds that they had no right to claim damages since under the *Coal Act 1938* and the *Coal Industry Nationalisation Act 1946* they now owned the coal and the ability to win it and were virtually claiming damages for actions taken by themselves. Other claimants were found to have been claiming for land they had previously sold. Nobody could prove their claim to my satisfaction and at a final meeting on 14 October 1972 the officer resigned and I was appointed in his stead at a salary of 5p per annum (which has never been requested).

The earlier correspondence of the officer was never handed over but certain documents that I subsequently received indicated that the operation of the Inclosure Act had supposedly been well tested and approved by Counsel in 1876, 1890, 1894, 1904, 1949, and 1971. It was also revealed that the officer appointed had not been observing the Statutory Rules of the Minister of Health no 932, made under section 83 of the *Local Government Act 1929*, as a result of which the levying of a rate in 1967 was ultra vires. It was also indicated that the officer had been making a charge to the N C B for part of the cost of bringing N C B coal from outside the Wakefield Inclosure Area to the surface at the N C B's Lofthouse Colliery and that the N C B had blithely paid on the tonnage.

The net amount of seven claimants in 1967 totalled £61 11s 11d, which included £18 10s 2d for the N C B and £24 7s 8d for British Rail. The officer had been collecting £125 a year plus expenses. By the *Coal Act 1938* all established coal reserves were purchased as a national asset. By the *Coal Industry Nationalisation Act 1946* all coal mining, coke ovens and other associated enterprises were brought under the control of the National Coal Board for the benefit of the people. Thus, should any further coal exploitation be undertaken without the terms of the *Wakefield Inclosure Act 1793* being invoked, then owners of property in and around Wakefield will not suffer the penalty of loss as inflicted prior to 1972.

And benefited householders...

The first reading of legal documents relating to property can be most interesting but when one observes that they usually have the same main details of type, date, parties and description of land, they are basically the same in structure, whether in the Ridings of Yorkshire or elsewhere, when they are conveyances of freehold property or long assignments of leasehold property. Just occasionally a will, or probate, would introduce fascinating features accompanying the transfer of property and land. An introduction to the Inclosure Acts and Awards, however, enables one to glimpse the origin of some titles rather than simply to discover who the line of previous owners might be.

In manorial England much property was of copyhold tenure and was transferred by copy of Court Roll in the Manor Court, and this was not registerable under the Yorkshire Registries Acts.

When first studying an Inclosure Award, such as came into my possession in 1973, it was immediately apparent that allotment of parts of the commons, or Lord's Waste, provided clear proof and root of title upon which all subsequent documents of transfer etc were based. In February 1978 I was consulted by a group of residents who had been served with notices by the County Council that their road was to be made up to the standard required for adoption and that they would be charged pro rata according to the length of their frontage. One of them was expected to pay £802. My careful study of the law indicated that they could avoid the charge if it could be proved that their road was a highway before 1835-6, in which case under the *Highways Act 1959* it was repairable at public expense. The *Wakefield Inclosure Award 1805* indicated that their road, Lingwell Nook Lane, had been set out as Lofthouse Gate Road, a private carriage road. (Figure 2) The Council held that if it was a private road then it was not a highway in 1836. A further study of the Award indicated both public and private roads, but it contained no mention of any restrictions. The challenge therefore was to find evidence from subsequent maps, and events, of derestriction. I was in an advantageous position to research every detail of every road defined, and concluded that all those public and private roads were similar highways from the outset. But 'Swinden's Theory', as it was termed by the opposition in Court was deemed insufficient. I had, however, found other more accessible 'private roads' in the same area which had been in use for many years as metalled highways and kept in good repair by the Council, giving some indication that they had

Figure 2. Lingwell Nook Lane, Lofthouse Gate, 1998. *Kate Taylor.*

Figure 3. Moor Road, Stanley, 1998. *Kate Taylor.*

never been restricted, I also found with Lingwell Nook Lane that gas lamps had been installed by the Council and that a Methodist chapel on the lane clearly indicated a highway. Similarly a railway bridge had been constructed over it and during its construction the lane was described as a highway. In late May 1980 the Court accepted the research as conclusive so the residents were absolved from responsibility.

Success in one case soon led to others, the next being a minor access to properties at Lee Moor, Wakefield. Again the same basic features were tested and discussed in Court, but detailed research into the history of the road was critical. The evidence of a post-box and gas lighting helped, but in this case the key factor was an examination of a part of the road which disclosed the use of an unusual green material for repairs. This was identified as smelting dross from Low Moor, Bradford, which had been brought in for use on other Council roads at Stanley in the earlier part of the twentieth century. At the end of the case, which lasted four days, residents at Moor Road (Cockpit Houses Road) were overjoyed at not having to pay the £15,000 repair bill plus costs (Figure 3). The cost to the County Council overall was £57,000.

Shortly following this success, the vicar of Gawthorpe asked for assistance as some half dozen residents were faced with road charges; their solicitors had advised them that they had no alternative but to pay and they agreed jointly that I should give them some guidance.

West Yorkshire Metropolitan County Council, which had succeeded the West Riding County Council in 1974, was most anxious to succeed and initially brought the case before the Magistrates' Court. The road, then called Chancery Lane, had been set out in the Ossett Inclosure Award 1807 as Shepherd Mill Road (Figure 4). The relevant plan was difficult to obtain but very extensive research into every aspect of the growth of Ossett, and particularly Gawthorpe, had to be undertaken. By this time I had more than 200 exhibits available for Counsel relative to 'Swinden's Theory' but once again the decisions rested on factors concerning the history of the use of the road in question. My most detailed researches and the study of old maps indicated that this tiny road, only about twelve feet in width, had been part of the main road to Leeds before better roads, and turnpike roads to the North East, had been cut through the masses of sandstone to provide what locals knew as Dewsbury Cutting. A further conclusive discovery was that it was also a very small part of a much earlier transpennine Roman track or road which had been used for generations, as shown on Bowen's map of 1775, linking Chester with Manchester, Castleshaw Roman Fort, Almondbury and Swillington with Boroughbridge. On one occasion in the quest for evidence I had seen an original 1762 Bowen's map

Figure 4. Chancery Lane, Ossett, 1998. *Kate Taylor*

of Yorkshire in an antique shop in Filey on a Sunday, but the shop was closed. Next day, 25 June 1982, however, I made another special journey and it was purchased ready for display in the Magistrates' Court. Incidentally at this time it was discovered that Chancery Lane was also part of Moor Road at Stanley. Was it a highway? Further research indicated that its continuation at Gawthorpe Lane had been the subject of repair indictments as the King's highway. The magistrates decided that before 1836 it was. In the Wakefield Crown Court, on appeal, attempts were made by leading counsel to confuse issues but again the examination of historical documents relating to Ossett and Dewsbury – on one occasion in a lunch break – provided rebuttal and the judge gave the verdict to the residents but he stated that he did not wish to hear any more attempts to have such matters brought before the courts. Once the matter of costs was settled the County Council came in for severe criticism for wasting ratepayers' money so in subsequent cases, after the same careful research, the Council's representatives examined my detailed evidence and in each case accepted the Council's responsibility for the respective roads. They included School Lane, Bunker's Hill and Rodger Lane in Wrenthorpe, Green Lane in Wakefield, and Church Road at Stanley, the latter being made up and adopted.

West Yorkshire County Council was disbanded in 1986 when the Metropolitan District Councils took over its responsibilities.

11. Shirts From Wakefield

by Kate Taylor

IN 1940 ISAAK DONNER AND HIS PARTNER, Frank Myers, set up a modest shirt-making enterprise at 126 Kirkgate, Wakefield.

Today, with its headquarters occupying a seven-acre site in Thornes Wharf Lane and with six factories, three on site and three remote, the Wakefield Shirt Group of Companies remains a family firm, employing 750 people (in December 1997) and selling over three million garments a year. Modern systems enable it to assemble a garment within two-and-a-half hours from start to finish and at any one time its warehouses hold a stock of 700,000 garments. The group now manufactures a substantial range of clothing including, for men, shirts for formal wear and day wear, fashion shirts and sports shirts, jeans and casual trousers, and for women shirts and blouses, dresses and soft suits, as well as career wear and workwear for both sexes.

It was Nazi oppression which led the thirty-five year old Isaak Donner to relinquish the family business in Vienna and to apply in 1939 for a licence to set up a manufacturing concern in England. It took him a year, during which time his son, Richard, was born whilst the family was living in Oxford. Donner was guided by the Board of Trade to the development areas of Yorkshire, in particular Barnsley, Huddersfield, Leeds and Wakefield, where school leavers, especially girls, were finding it difficult to obtain work. At Wakefield Labour Exchange Donner was given a 'red carpet' reception. He was told of the closure of Benefit Footwear Ltd, formerly the Public Benefit Boot and Shoe Company, and the possibility of using its Kirkgate premises.(Figure 1) The footwear concern had been incorporated in 1897 with Brow Dickinson and C C Graham as its directors and in the same year it had taken over the Kirkgate property of boot manufacturer William Franklin.[1]

Work began in the midsummer of 1940 in a single room. The first order, for twelve dozen shirts, was placed by the Leeds outfitters, Shiphams.[2] Steady expansion meant that Donner and Myers were able to buy the whole of the Kirkgate premises (Figure 1). Myers, who had been based in Berlin, had also fled Hitler's persecution and, unable to obtain a licence himself, had sought an association with

Donner. Their partnership lasted until Myers' death in May 1968.[3]

During the war years, when rayon made from British woodpulp was the most readily obtained fabric and imported cotton was scarce, output was mainly of women's shirt blouses. It was shortly after the war that the famous Double Two shirt came into being. Men returning from war service wanted shirts with integral soft collars like the ones their American allies had worn. But collars wore out long before the body of the shirt. Donner invented and patented the *Double Two* shirt with the idea of giving the garment a second life by providing each one with an additional collar and set of cuffs which could easily be stitched into place, hence the company's name (Figure 2).

Donner now regularly took a stand at the British Industrial Fairs at Earls Court (Figures 3, 4 and 5).

Terylene, the first man-made fibre to be knitted, supplemented

Figure 1. The premises in Kirkgate, on the corner of George Street, where the Wakefield Shirt Company was originally based. *Courtesy the Wakefield Shirt Company.*

cotton fabrics from 1951 when Isaak Donner was able to show his first two Terylene shirts on the first day of the British Industries Fair after a memorable scramble to obtain exclusive rights to the remarkable new fabric from its developers, ICI.

In 1955 with orders booming and a labour force of 500, the company moved into Portobello Mills in Thornes Wharf Lane, adding a canteen and running special buses from the centre of Wakefield for the workpeople.[4] The greater space allowed for a modern production system. (Figure 6) The new site, beside the Calder and Hebble Navigation, had been in industrial use since the 1790s when Thomas Mellin built a dyehouse and stoving house there. In the 1840s Joseph Holdsworth redeveloped the site for the growing industry of worsted spinning. After a number of changes of occupant, the mill was bought by Joseph Wade, a Morley cloth manufacturer, who in 1861 established Wakefield's first large-scale cloth manufacturing firm there.[5] The Wakefield Shirt Company bought the mill complex from Wade's successors for £18,500 in

Figure 2a. An early advertisement for a Double Two blouse. *Courtesy the Wakefield Shirt Company.*

Figure 2b. An early advertisement for the Double Two shirt. *Courtesy the Wakefield Shirt Company.*

March 1954.[6] Over the next twenty years the company systematically acquired properties in Wellington Street (including the former maltkiln of M Sanderson) and to the west of Portobello Mills up to the railway viaduct to consolidate their site.[7]

Demand for non-iron garments led the company to create Europe's first permanent-press shirt, made from 100% cotton, in 1965 and marketed as 'White Light'.[8]

In June 1966, when the workforce had risen to 800 and the company was one of the top three shirt-manufacturing concerns in the country, George Darling, minister of state at the Board of Trade, opened the company's new 50,000 square feet warehouse in Thornes Wharf Lane.[9]

Diversification came first in 1968 when the Wakefield Shirt Company acquired the shares of the long-established firm of William Sugden and Sons, known particularly for its Jet Jeans, W L B Workwear, and Top Twenty shirts. The business had been founded by William Sugden as a tailoring concern in Railway Street, Cleckheaton in 1869. His two eldest sons embarked on shirt-making at the back of his shop in 1896. Three years later they moved to Water Lane Mills,. Cleckheaton. Expansion came quite rapidly with the opening of a factory in Barnsley in 1904 where a new factory was built in 1912. In November 1924 the company, which had been

Figure 3. Her Majesty the Queen visiting the Double Two stand at a trade fair in the 1950s.

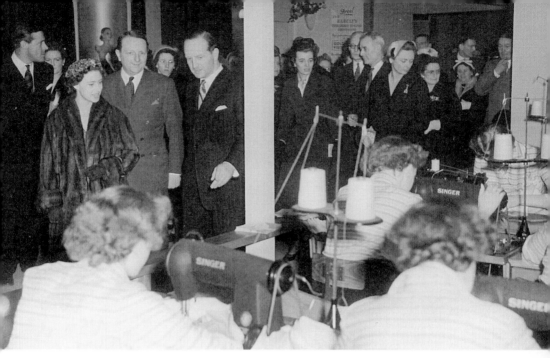

Figure 4. Her Royal Highness Princess Margaret visiting the Double Two stand at the British Industrial Fair, Earl's Court in 1948. Sales Director Charles Burnham is pointing out features of the shirts. *Courtesy Wakefield Shirt Company.*

manufacturing in Wakefield too since 1911, bought the Albion Works in Vicarage Street, Wakefield, which had been built in 1871 for the family business of William Nicholson and Sons, who were printers and publishers and who pioneered cheap books. Nicholsons' was wound up in 1921. In 1957 Sugden's, by then producing the newly-popular jeans as well as shirts and workwear, bought a small unit at Wath-upon-Dearne where they built a new factory in 1965.[10]

The 'family' nature of the group was maintained after the takeover. David and John Sugden, descendants of the founder of the firm, joined Isaak Donner and, by then, his son Richard in the management of what then became the Wakefield Shirt Group of Companies with Sugden's retaining its name as a subsidiary. Richard Donner was educated at Wakefield's Queen Elizabeth Grammar School, Leeds University, where he read Textiles and Economics, and Harvard Business School, and he joined the company, as a 'dog's body', in 1963. After working as the production manager, in marketing, and in the buying of fabrics, he became the group managing director in the 1980s. Richard's son John joined the group in 1995. Isaak Donner remains the group chairman (Figure 7).

Only a year after acquiring Sugden's, and after pressure from

Figure 5. All eyes (!), including those of Arthur Askey, on Double Two shirts at the British Industrial Fair at Earl's Court 1948.
Courtesy Wakefield Shirt Company.

Figure 6. Production at Thornes Wharfe Lane in the 1950s.
Courtesy Wakefield Shirt Company.

Wakefield Corporation which feared losing the city's major department store, the Wakefield Shirt Company expanded into retailing when it purchased Kingswell's which then occupied a substantial site in Northgate and Westmorland Street. Kingswell's had been a family business since 1898 until its takeover by the Lancashire-based Lewis group of fashion stores in 1967.[11] A part of the premises had, by the 1850s, been that of Harnew and Glover, retailing drapery and hosiery. This had been succeeded by King and when W H Kingswell came as a partner in 1875 had become King and Kingswell. For some years Kingswell's was managed by Isaak Donner's daughter, Judy. In 1971 the Wakefield Shirt Company expanded the store, taking premises lying between Cross Square and the Bull Ring. The Northgate premises were closed in 1986 but the Cross Street shop still flourishes.[12] The group now has thirty retail outlets.

Technological innovation is regarded by the company as fundamental to maintaining its success. In 1959-60 the company installed a modern production line brought in from Sweden where Richard Donner had gained work experience whilst still at school. Administration has been handled by a computer since the company installed its first IBM System/3 in 1968 which was used for order analysis, stock, credit and shipping control, packing note production, invoicing and the preparation of customer statements, the calculation of salesmen's commissions, and the production of order and despatch statistics. In 1979 the company upgraded to an IBM System/34 and in 1990 to an IBM AS400. In 1980 the company entered the field of computer-aided design (CAD) with one of the first Hughes systems for marker-making and pattern design. In 1982 a Mitsubishi computer-aided design system was installed for fabric design and garment-concept design (Figures 8 and 9).

A visit by Richard Donner to Japan in November 1978 has resulted in the company's shirts being manufactured under licence by the Teijan Trading Company in Osaka since 1979. In the mid 1980s Richard started licensed shirt production in India with the Jainson's Group. Since a large part of this production was for Russia, sales have

Figure 7. Three generations of the Donner family, Isaak (seated), Richard (right) and Richard's son, John. *Courtesy Wakefield Shirt Company.*

dropped since the break up of the Russian empire and the breaking of the link between the Indian rupee and the Russian rouble.

The 1980s saw continued expansion. In 1987, under Sugden's umbrella, the group acquired L J and M Refson of Sunderland, manufacturers of women's uniforms and career wear, and a year later it bought a further shirt factory, the West Riding Shirt Company, in Wombwell.

Then in 1990 the group founded *ThreadNeedle* which distributes corporate clothing and can provide up to 60,000 customized garments a week for such companies as British Gas, the A A, the prison service, British Petroleum, Boots, GNER, Scotrail, Scottish and Manweb Electricity, MEB and Elizabeth Arden among others, and for police, fire and ambulance services. At the same time the group opened a modern suite of offices in Thornes Lane.

The acquisition of a 50% interest in *Mansworld* in York in 1994 led to the formation of a chain of factory outlet stores which by 1997 numbered five with an annual turnover of £8m.

The company takes a pride in its role both in the local community and in charitable work. This might involve anything from taking part in the Macmillan Nurses' record-breaking coffee morning, and supporting Wakefield Hospice, to sending a large consignment of shirts and blouses to the British Red Cross for shipping to Mozambique and three ambulances full of clothing to Rumanian orphanages. In the early 1960s the company partnered Wakefield

Figure 8. Computer terminal on the automated Eaton line system for shirts at Thornes Wharf Lane headquarters. *Courtesy Wakefield Shirt Company.*

Corporation, in what was possibly the first green venture between a local authority and a commercial concern, in land acquisition, tree-planting and landscaping in Wellington Street and Tadman Street. In 1968 the company supported Wakefield Civic Society's tree-planting scheme on Thornes Wharf. The Group is a corporate member of the Yorkshire Wildlife Trust and Richard Donner serves as its vice-chairman.

In July 1992 British athletes at the opening of the Olympic games in Barcelona wore *Double Two* shirts.[13] Later that year the company took its first order for shirts for Moscow and St.Petersburg.[14] Subsequently retail customers were found in Latvia, Lithuania, Belarus, Ukraine and Slovenia, adding to the company's traditional markets in Western Europe, the Middle East, Africa and South America. Overall the company now sells its *Double Two* brand products in over forty countries. Originating in Wakefield, to escape from one of the most oppressive regimes of twentieth century Europe, the Group can be regarded as truly international in its outlook and reach.

Acknowledgments

The writer would like to thank Isaak and Richard Donner for their assistance in the preparation of this account.

Notes and References

1. West Riding Registry of Deeds, 1897 Vol 32 p803 and 1898 Vol 50 p385
2. *Wakefield Express*, 13 November 1992
3. Obituary, Wakefield Express, 25 May 1968.
4. *Wakefield Express,* 29 October 1955
5. J Goodchild, Wakefield and Wool, 1981.
6. West Riding Registry of Deeds 1954 Vol 40, p1003.
7. West Riding Registry of Deeds 1968 Vol 166 p522
8. *Wakefield Express*, 8 June 1990.
9. Ibid. 23 July 1966.
10. K Taylor (ed), *Wakefield District Heritage* Vol II, 1979, pp134-5, and promotional material published by the Wakefield Shirt Group of Companies.
11. *Wakefield Express*, 29 July 1967, 22 February 1969, 8 September 1972
12. *Ibid.* 14 February 1986.
13. *Ibid.* 24 July 1992.
14. *Ibid.* 13 November 1992.

Figure 9. Shirt production prior to the latest innovations.

Courtesy Wakefield Shirt Company.

12. THE CREAM OF HOSPICES: THE FOUNDINGS OF WAKEFIELD HOSPICE.

by Alan Kirkbright

Figure 1. A twelve year old schoolgirl devised a logo for future use by the hospice: a pair of caring hands supporting a precious heart at the close of day.

THE TERM HOSPICE DATES BACK to the Middle Ages. It was a type of hostel, typically attached to a monastery, to provide shelter for travellers and the needy. The meaning of the word has changed in modern times, following the work done by Dr Cicely Saunders, a director of St Christopher's Hospice in London. The prime purpose of a hospice today is to provide terminal care facilities to help patients and their families cope with death and dying.

The need for a hospice in Wakefield was identified by five nursing staff, four of whom were based at Clayton Hospital. All of them nursed on acute surgical wards or were in charge of departments dealing with patients in need of specialist medical and nursing care. Their duties inevitably brought them into contact with the dying and they considered that more palliative measures for the terminally ill could be provided by the special nursing care available only at a hospice. Many such patients were referred to St Gemma's Hospice in Leeds which had opened in 1978 and where a special unit dealing with the terminally ill patient was already operative. To help St Gemma's financially they held coffee mornings and jumble sales, sending the proceeds of their efforts to the hospice to help towards its upkeep. But the transfer of patients from Wakefield to Leeds presented problems for visiting relatives, many of whom were elderly. It was at this juncture that the pressing need for a hospice in Wakefield was realised and in the summer of 1982 the venture got under way.

On 3 November 1982 the inaugural meeting was held at Clayton Hospital. There were 46 people present. A steering committee was formed consisting of Marie Sullivan, Area Nursing Officer (chairman), Joyce Swann, staff nurse, Clayton Hospital (vice-chairman), Phyllis Chapman, staff nurse, Clayton Hospital (secretary), Max Dawson (treasurer) and Tony McVicar (legal adviser) together with Joan O'Leary, ward sister, Clayton Hospital,

Barbara Wain, departmental sister, Clayton Hospital, Olive Carley, nursing sister, Ann Thomas, Ann Bastow and Ruth Stewart. In mid-November the legal adviser, Tony McVicar, was requested to apply to the Charity Commission to register the embryo organisation as a charity. Charitable status was granted in June 1983, enabling the organisation to benefit from deeds of covenant (Figure 1).

The need for a hospice was indisputable. The chairman of the appeal fund, Marie Sullivan, confirmed that the will was there and all that was required was lots of money – initially £250,000 of it to build the hospice and about £150,000 a year to run it.

The Wakefield Area Health Authority when discussing the project agreed that the scheme was most laudable but

> *in the foreseeable future, with little or no funds available, it was not envisaged that the Authority would be in a position to make any financial contribution unless monies were diverted from other areas of patient care.*

Despite the lack of financial support from the Health Authority, the people of Wakefield and district, undeterred by this rebuff for their cause, pressed ahead with their efforts and continued to raise funds for the project. By March 1983 about £5,000 had been raised from the proceeds from jumble sales, coffee mornings and bring-and-buy sales. Numerous support groups were organised throughout the district and by their efforts the fund continued to swell. But even at this stage some members of the public doubted the viability of the project.

A public meeting was held in the Minor Hall, Unity House, when Major the Rt Hon Lord St Oswald was invited to become president. Not only did he accept this office, but he kindly offered the use of Nostell Priory for fund-raising activities. Several people accepted invitations to become vice-presidents and more support groups were formed in different geographical areas of the city. A new committee was formed which met at the home of the Provost of Wakefield, Very Rev John Allen, and Mrs Allen. Church groups became actively involved in the appeal. Industrial organisations were asked for support in 'payroll' giving. Sanderson and Clayton's was the first firm to take this on board.

After seven months £13,000 had been raised. This was supplemented by the proceeds from sponsored walks, swims, and parachute jumps, the sale of goods from stalls at various fayres, and from collecting boxes throughout the city. Support came also from Masonic sources and from a fashion parade at Queen Elizabeth

Grammar School, as well as other activities.

In time there was a change in administrative personnel: in June 1983 Marie Sullivan resigned as chairman and was replaced by Edwin Hirst.

The first hospice shop was opened in Marygate in January 1984. Funds were augmented by donations from 57 Friends of the Hospice; by March 1984 the number had increased to 132. The bank balance had climbed to £64,000. Income from the hospice shops had increased the coffers by £9,300. Relatives of those who died requested that donations be sent to the hospice treasurer in lieu of flowers.

The Yorkshire Bank ofered the movement shop premises in Northgate where Mary McAuliffe groomed members as fashion models.

In June 1984 Roy Cusworth became legal adviser. Further invaluable advice came from the support teams from St Gemma's in Leeds and St Luke's, Sheffield.

A book of remembrance in which the names of the dead could be entered was presented by Christine Ellis and her Community Entertainers.

By November 1984, £100,000 had been collected, of which £20,000 had been raised from the hospice shops.

The search for suitable premises was accelerating. Several sites and premises were visited but for a variety of reasons they were considered unsuitable. In the meantime fund-raising efforts continued unabated. A Christmas Fayre at Treacy Hall, cycle marathons and the inaugural Friendship Supper by the St John's group were noteworthy contributors. Regrettably Lord St Oswald, who had contributed in no small way, died before the hospice was erected.

By April 1985 the fund had reached £126,000. The brother of the late Lord St Oswald succeeded him as president and continued to

Figure 2. The Hospice Shop in Cross Street, 1998. *Kate Taylor.*

support the appeal. The Yorkshire Bank kindly offered premises in Cross Street in exchange for the Northgate shop (Figure 2). The appeal chairman, Edwin Hirst, resigned for business reasons and was replaced by the legal adviser, Roy Cusworth. The Rt Reverend David Hope, recently appointed as Bishop of Wakefield, offered the grounds of Bishop's Lodge, Sandal, for a garden party, which has now become an annual event.

Nothing succeeds like success! The ever-increasing revenue from the shops necessitated the purchase, in January 1986, of transport to collect goods donated by the public. Alan Willey volunteered to drive it. In May the hospice acquired office accommodation in Bank Street. There were many offers of help and Ann Stride, along with others, worked there voluntarily three days a week.

December 1986 brought the highlight of the year. The fund had reached £300,000 and the long search for a site for the hospice came to an end. At first the buildings standing on two acres of land at the former Newmillerdam Colliery were considered suitable. However when the Wakefield Health Authority agreed to offer land close to Pinderfields Hospital, it was considered to be a better site. Consequently Roy Cusworth entered into meaningful discussions with Sir Jack Smart, chairman of the Health Authority, who now expressed enthusiasm for supporting the project.

Stuart Robinson was appointed as project manager and in March 1987 there were further negotiations with the Local Authority. Edwin Hirst returned to become the appeals fund manager. His help was invaluable. As a respected member of the business community he persuaded many of his associates during his period in office to make generous donations to the Appeal Fund. At the same time fund raising continued with numerous events arranged by organisations across a wide spectrum of the community.

August 1987 saw another change of personnel. Kath Robinson, who had worked in all the hospice shops, continued the sterling work of Mary McAuliffe who left Wakefield. The shops became the foremost means of fundraising, with a staff of about 30 working on a voluntary basis each week. The following month a meeting with the architect, Peter Marshall, took place when the outline plans of the hospice were discussed. The summer of 1988 was earmarked for the commencement of building.

The hopes and aspirations of many who had laboured hard for their goal were realised on 30 July 1988. The turf was cut by the president, Lord St Oswald. Trees were planted by Sir Jack Smart, the Mayor Councillor Parkinson, and the former nurses whose vision

Figure 3. The cream of hospices: Wakefield Hospice where building was completed in December 1989. *Alan Kirkbright.*

was nearing fulfilment. In December 1988 Judith Powell was appointed as matron to commence her duties in 1989. Further appointments included Barbara Baker as administrator and later Dr Paresh Gajjar as medical director.

The construction of the hospice was completed in December 1989 (Figure 3).

In his book about hospices, Martyn Lewis, the popular broadcaster and author of *Tears and Smiles,* described the Wakefield hospice as 'the cream of hospices'. What better commendation could one have hoped for?

The cost of construction was approximately £920,000. Furnishing and fitting cost a further £60,000, and the annual running cost was estimated at £450,000. These figures are in marked contrast to those suggested during the early days as the target to aim for. The hospice received a Registration Certificate in the spring of 1990 and became operational to receive 'day care' patients on 26 March. On 1 April a thanksgiving service was held in Wakefield Cathedral for all those who had worked unstintingly to fulfil the vision of a hospice for Wakefield. The original 46 had swelled to several hundred active supporters. The first patient was admitted the following day, 2 April 1990.

A plaque in the reception area of the hospice commemorates the official opening by the Duchess of Norfolk on 21 August 1990. Printed below her name are five others, those of the five dedicated nurses whose idea to ease the pain of the dying became a reality. One of those, Joan O'Leary, a former sister on A C 2 Ward at Clayton Hospital, was herself nursed for a short time at St Gemma's Hospice prior to her untimely death from leukaemia. The Wakefield hospice

Figure 4. A group at the official opening of the hospice by the Duchess of Norfolk on 21 August 1990. Left to right, the president, Lord St. Oswald, Joyce Swann, Phyllis Chapman, Barbara Wain, Mrs. O'Leary, the Duchess of Norfolk, and Olive Carley. *Alan Kirkbright.*

serves as a reminder to others of the care and compassion for the sick and dying shown by this hospital sister during her long nursing career. It was typical of the sensitivity of the hospice movement that they should invite Sister O'Leary's sister-in-law from Killarney to take her place at the opening ceremony (Figure 4).

A more professional approach to fund raising and to day-to-day administration was now essential. The first step was to form a company limited by guarantee and the hospice has now assumed the title of Wakefield Hospice Ltd. Previously all decisions were taken by the Appeal Fund Council. This was a body elected annually from the Friends of the Hospice, who pay an annual subscription. With the formation of the company, the Council members became Hospice Company members and they elected trustees to administer the day-to-day running of the hospice. The trustees are called the Council of Management and their current chairman (February 1998) is Graham Bird, cancer consultant. The Appeal Fund Council is primarily concerned with overseeing fund-raising activities. It still maintains an important 'watchdog' role, including retaining responsibility for the supervision of fourteen support groups throughout the district, who, through voluntary efforts, raise about

£70,000 annually. Council members meet quarterly to receive reports from the Council of Management. The present chairman of the Appeal Fund Council is Margaret Davies who actively liaises with the trustees.

When fund-raising became a commercial venture (selling goods purchased for sale at the hospice shops, as opposed to voluntary fund-raising), a subsidiary of the hospice company was formed. This is the Wakefield Hospice (Fund-Raising) Company Ltd, under the chairmanship of Mr.Bird, chairman of the trustees. Four hospice shops, two in Wakefield, one in Horbury and one in Ossett, continue to provide a considerable source of revenue.

In September 1997 Helen Knowles was replaced as fundraising manager by Karen Elliott. Volunteers are always need to help at the many events promoted by this part of the organisation.

There are currently eight beds in use by the terminally ill. A further sixteen patients who are ill with terminal disease can be accommodated each week as 'day care' patients (Figure 5). The aims of the 'day care' service are to provide the highest standard of care, to control pain and other symptoms, considering the patient as a person with social, emotional and spiritual needs, to work with, supplement and support existing services and facilities available in the community, and to support families during this time and in their bereavement.

On 14 March 1983 the local press observed

The Wakefield area has always been generous, energetic and imaginative in fund-raising. As the need for a hospice touches all ages and kinds of people, so all ages and kinds of people can help to make the dream of a hospice a reality.

The continued search for yet more funds remains unabated.

In the 1996/7 Annual Report the income was shown as £1,005,824 against an expenditure of £813,364. The hospice is currently appealing for £1,000,000 extra revenue. This will increase

Figure 5. The day care centre. The chapel, which serves all religious denominations, is on the right of the picture. *Alan Kirkbright.*

the number of people able to receive in-patient care from eight to sixteen. Work started in April 1998 and is on target for completion in April 1999. The new extension will include overnight-stay bedrooms and a treatment bathroom. The initial parameters of treating only those people with terminal illness have widened to include those patients with a chronic illness whose families are in need of respite from the pressures of dealing with it.

By February 1998 1,653 terminally ill patients had received palliative treatment enabling them to die with dignity. Several hundred more have passed through the hospice's portals for day care.

An excerpt from the leaflet *Caring for You* reads:

> *Wakefield Hospice respects the rights of patients to equal concern and attention, whatever their gender, race, class, culture, religious belief, age, sexuality, lifestyle or degree of physical ability. We treat patients with respect and dignity,. taking their physical and emotional, spiritual and social needs seriously throughout their lives whatever the prognosis.*

These aspirations are achieved in an atmosphere of warmth and care within the comfortable furnishings of the hospice at no personal cost to the patients themselves. The cost to the hospice for in-patient care is £1,851 15p per week and for day care is £39 per patient. Its viability is dependent on donations from benefactors both great and small. Those members of the movement who collect from shoppers in precinct and supermarket testify to the generosity of all social groups and emphasise that the 'widow's mite' makes a very substantial contribution to this worthwhile cause.

The valuable service the hospice provides was recognised by Her Majesty the Queen during her visit there on 22 March 1992.

This is a fairy tale of the hopes and aspirations of five hospital nurses come true. The public support for the hospice has been phenomenal. The unstinting support by volunteers was recognised by the committee at a public meeting at Queen Elizabeth Grammar School in 1997 when badges were presented to those who had served the cause in fund-raising activities for five and for ten years. It is not possible to name the countless numbers of people and organisations which have contributed to the remarkable success of this venture. Whilst their names may have been omitted, their contribution is manifest in the bricks and mortar of a hospice they helped to create in the service of others.

13. LOFTHOUSE PARK

by Peter I Wood

IN AN EFFORT TO INCREASE ITS PROFITS Yorkshire (West Riding) Electric Tramway Company Ltd decided to open a tramway amusement park, which would be the first of its kind in Great Britain, through its own subsidiary company, Lofthouse Park Ltd established with the directors from the parent company.[1] The tramway company was the only one in the Dewsbury and Wakefield area to construct from its own resources a full tramway system, complete with its own generating station and plant for converting the generated three-phase 6,300 volts to a direct current of 500-550 volts.[2] Other tram companies followed the general pattern of leasing their equipment from various manufacturers of trams and tramways. The company was registered to take over the running of the tramway system on 4 April 1905, and did so from an earlier company, the Wakefield and District Light Railways, that had laid down the lines and built the plant to begin running trams for the general public on 15 August 1904.[3]

A 60-acre plot of land was purchased to create an entertainment centre at Lofthouse. This site would be located on land between what is now the M62 and Lofthouse Gate on the eastern side of the A61, where the present West Yorkshire Mechanical Engineering Depot is situated (Figure 1). From 1800 the land had been in the ownership of Benjamin Dealtry who built Lofthouse Hall in 1801. Dealtry was a one-time barrister of the Inner Temple and later a magistrate of the West Riding of Yorkshire.[4] On his death the land was inherited by his son who rented the estate to Josiah Ramskill, and on the son's death it went to Benjamin Dealtry's two daughters. The estate was later purchased by Joseph Charlesworth. In 1907 the tramway company's subsidiary. Lofthouse Park Ltd, bought both Hawthorn Cottage and Lofthouse Park from members of the Charlesworth family.

The company quickly started creating the leisure park and buildings and was able to open to the paying public on 3 June 1908 (Figure 2). A double siding, capable of holding at least eight trams, was created on the western side of the park so that there would be no interruption to through tram traffic while the expected crowds boarded trams or alighted at the park entrances.[5] Mr.Andrews, who

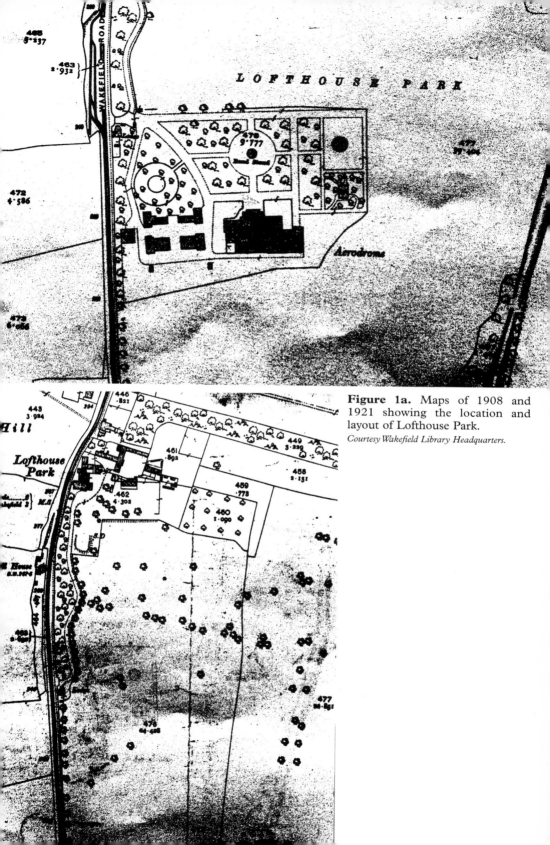

Figure 1a. Maps of 1908 and 1921 showing the location and layout of Lofthouse Park.

Courtesy Wakefield Library Headquarters.

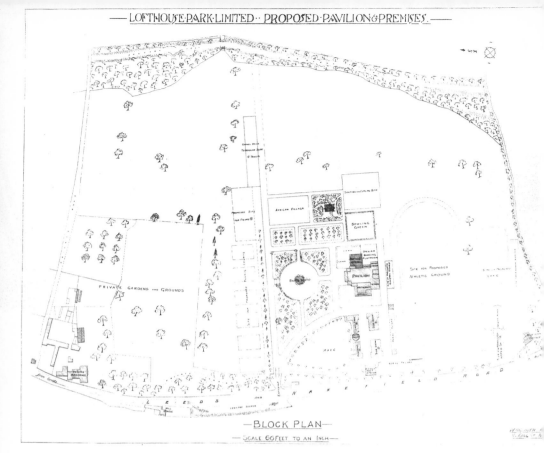

—BLOCK PLAN—
—SCALE 66 FEET TO AN INCH—

Figure 1b. Plan by the Wakefield architect, W H Glover, for the grounds.

Courtesy Wakefield Library Headquarters.

Figure 2. The advertisement in the *Wakefield Express* for the opening of Lofthouse Park on 3 June 1908.

lived for some time in The Mansion at the top of Lofthouse Hill, which was on the northern boundary of the park, was secretary of the Wakefield and District Light Railway Company. He is quoted in the local press as saying that the site of 60 acres was well wooded and that many of the trees would be saved to make sheltered and shaded walks.

At the entrance to the park, a decorative and illuminated arch that spanned the roadway was next to an almost circular

Figure 3. Lofthouse Park pavilion. The figure in the foreground is Henry Horner, the park warden. *Courtesy of Raymond Colley.*

building, Lodge Cottage, in which lived a retired policeman, Henry Horner, who combined the duties of warden with those of caretaker.

A large wooden pavilion of oriental design, complete with a gilded dome and a roof studded with coloured bulbs, surmounted with two turrets, could hold 1,000 people (Figure 3). This pavilion, or concert hall, similar to one at Yarmouth, had a stage and all the equipment necessary for live performances; it also had a grill room, cloak room and offices. At one side of the stage was an orchestra alcove, from which visiting orchestras could provide music for dancers in the hall or, if the weather permitted, dancers using an outside floor. Wakefield men were employed in the design and construction of the park and its pavilion. W H Glover was the architect, plumbing was by Alderman Atkinson's company and the painting was carried out by Turner and Son. The fact that the whole construction seemed to have been mainly of timber might account for the swiftness of erection but to have been able to admit the paying public less than a month after design and building was quite remarkable. At one side of the hall was a large conservatory, going under the grand title of Winter Gardens, and on the other side were refreshment rooms staffed by a corps of male cooks led by an experienced chef from Spiers and Pond. The Winter Gardens was a glass and iron building, liberally filled with palm trees and plants from hotter climes, in which refreshments could be enjoyed at black or green painted iron tables, while reclining on wooden chairs.

Outside was the large, brick band-stand, illuminated with 600 electric light bulbs, under the care of an Italian, Signor G D La Camera. He had been resident in England for 35 years and had conducted before royalty. The band-stand would contain the 'military style' resident band, unless an invitation band was playing. On the opening day the company paid for the band of the Yorkshire Hussars, and other well-known bands would perform at later dates. (Figure 4.).

Further entertainment could be found either at the 50-yard square bowling green or on the open-air skating rink ('rough skaters will not be allowed'). The instructor was Emma Horner, daughter of the caretaker, and later Doris Mottershead, a daughter of the manager who had been employed from February 1911.

Behind the pavilion was a 'puzzle garden', or maze, made from six to seven foot privet hedging, a 'native village' peopled by inhabitants of the Philippines, and many side-shows and catch-penny stalls, the largest being the stall where elephant rides could be obtained. There were a helter-skelter and two aerial glides where patrons could either sit on chairs or hang from a T-bar to glide along a rope to the ground. For the not so brave there were the House of Mirrors and Kelly's House, a fun house of unexpected happenings. One of the exceptional entertainments provided was to watch an open-top

Figure 4. The bandstand at Lofthouse Park.   *From the collection of Norman Ellis.*

touring car roll down a steep ramp fifteen feet from the ground and travel some twenty feet into buffers at the bottom, still ten feet from the ground, turn a full somersault and land on its wheels on a large mattress with its driver and occupants unhurt and in place.

The grounds of the park were laid out with pathways winding their way amongst trees and flower-beds. At the time of opening plans were well advanced for a boating lake, a water chute, a motor railway, an athletic field and even football and cricket pitches.

An unusual feature of the park was the glass-covered sub-station where one could watch the rotary convertors generating the direct current for the track and for all flood-lighting and the 40,000 or 50,000 fairy lights.

The company ran a special advertising car for the opening, at which passengers retaining their ticket could get into the park at a reduced fee. The price of a return ticket was 8d from Wakefield but during March 1909 the same fare was extended to Sandal, Agbrigg and Horbury. From March 1911 a through return ticket from Dewsbury could be obtained for a shilling. There were also 'specials' running from Leeds to the park. Children travelled at a reduced price and every Monday afternoon special entertainments were provided for them.

On three evenings each week the park was to have a firework show, with fireworks from Brock, the London manufacturer (Figure 5). Special events would be planned for public and school holidays. The park even offered the latest entertainment in Bioscope picture shows with Herbert Whitaker as projectionist.

On 23 June 1908 Lofthouse Park Ltd entertained tramway managers from across the country and many local dignitaries with a tour, lunch, and an account of how and why the park had been envisaged.

The programme of events on the opening day was to last from

Figure 5. Another advertisement of 1908 announcing firework displays by Messrs. Brock.

LOFTHOUSE PARK
(Midway between Leeds and Wakefield).

CONTINUOUS ROUND OF ENTERTAIN-MENTS DAILY, from 11 a.m. to 10 p.m. Expensive Engagement of First-class MILITARY BAND. Conductor, Signor G. D. La Camera. Two Performances daily throughout the season.

3 DISPLAYS OF FIREWORKS WEEKLY by Messrs. Brock, of the Crystal Palace, London. Refreshment Caterers: Spiers and Pond, Ltd., London. Full Licence. Dining. Grill, Tea Rooms, etc. Large Pavilion. Winter Gardens. Immense Outdoor Dancing Platform. Illuminations and Numerous Permanent Attractions. Variety Entertainments in the Pavilion. Native Igorrote Village. High-class Pierrots. Bioscope Pictures. Fun Factory, and all kinds of Amusements in the Grounds.

FIREWORK DAYS: WEDNESDAYS and SATURDAYS.

Free Admission by Return Tram Tickets on Wednesdays up to Four o'clock; after Four o'clock, 6d.

DAYLIGHT FIREWORKS EVERY MONDAY AFTERNOON.

Admission Charges:—Mondays, Tuesdays, Thursdays, and Fridays: Free Admission by Return Tram Ticket; without return ticket 3d. Tram Cars direct from Leeds, Wakefield, and all parts to the Park Gate Entrance every few minutes.

LOFTHOUSE PARK.

Under the Direction of Mr. Arthur Corelli.
OPEN DAILY, from 11 a.m. to 10 p.m.
At 3 and 7.   Bright and Diversified
VARIETY & PIERROT ENTERTAINMENTS
FREE in the GRAND PAVILION.
DANCING every evening after the show.
Carlton Temperance Prize Band, Saturdays.
Change of Artistes and Programme Weekly.

NEW SUMMER SKATING RINK.

Perfect Rock Maple Surface, as smooth as ice
SESSIONS : 11 to 1, 2.30 to 5, 7 to 10.
Band afternoon and evening.
Ladies FREE to Park for Morning Session.
Ball-bearing Skates : 'Ladies' 6d. ; Gent's 1s.
For the benefit of all Patrons, Strict Order
is maintained. Rough Skating not allowed.
Persons negligently attired not admitted.

Free Puzzle Garden, Side Shows, Helter
Skelter, Aerial Flight, Houp-la, and all sorts
of Attractive Amusement Devices.

ADMITTANCE (To See Everything) 3D.
Gala Days excepted.
REFRESHMENTS of every kind : Full Licence.

SATURDAY, JULY 3rd, at 2.30.
GREAT BRASS BAND CONTEST.
Special Attractions.   Admission as usual.

Figure 6. An advertisement of July 1909 advertising the roller-skating rink
and a brass band contest at Lofthouse Park.

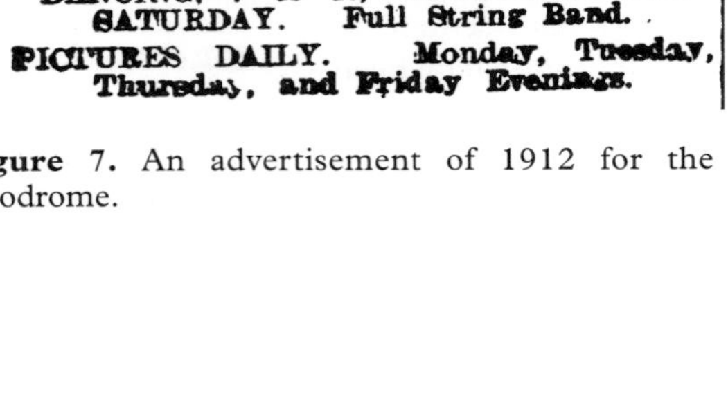

YORKSHIRE AERODROME,
LOFTHOUSE PARK.

FLYING, WEDNESDAY and SATURDAY
(Weather permitting).
DANCING, 7 to 10, WEDNESDAY and
SATURDAY.   Full String Band.
PICTURES DAILY.   Monday, Tuesday,
Thursday, and Friday Evenings.

Figure 7. An advertisement of 1912 for the
aerodrome.

11am to 10pm and these hours seem to have been the norm, certainly during the lighter nights.

On the first August Bank Holiday no less than three bands provided music while acrobats, gymnasts, vocalists, comedians, dancers, comedy cyclists, pierrots, and marionettes entertained. A jujitsu wrestling competition was arranged between county champions. On the sports field there were 'old English' sports in which adults and children were encouraged to participate.

The company went from strength to strength during the early years, obviously confident in their appeal to the paying public passing through the gates. The Easter programme 1909 illustrates the desire of the park management to give good value. In the hall for the first hour was a magic show, followed by an hour of entertainment with Miss Lil Sinclair (comedienne and dancer), The Evalos (comedy jugglers and gymnasts), Long Amos (eccentric character comedian), Piccolo and Fiori (clowns) and Mr 'E' (original humourist and storyteller). The performances were repeated from 3.30pm to 4.30pm and again from 6.30pm to 7.30pm. Throughout the day there was 'rinking in the pavilion' and dancing in the ballroom. One could also watch the pierrots, the Brothers Zarno, and the Merry Mascots, or listen to the Leeds Model Prize Band. The cost for eleven hours of all this? Just sixpence. (Figure 6)

In July 1910 there were balloon ascents and parachute descents; both would have an impact on the public in the next four or five years. The following year Lofthouse Park was advertising itself as Yorkshire Aerodrome with flying on Wednesdays and Saturdays (weather permitting).[7] The principal establishment amongst these early fliers was the company set up by Harold and Robert Blackburn.[8] This was, of couse, the Blackburn Aeroplane Company, which erected a large hangar for its monoplanes at the lower end of the park. The pilots were building their own aircraft somewhere in the park, so a test flight would have been an exciting event to watch. Pilots would try to develop flying techniques and it was possibly at Lofthouse that B C Hucks, a winner of several daily paper flying awards, performed the first 'looping the loop' aerobatics. With these early aeroplanes, made from canvas over a bamboo structure, and with primitive petrol engines, accidents were inevitable. One craft failed to lift off and crashed though the hedge on the eastern side of the park while another plane crashed at Lee Moor in a rhubarb field (Figure 7).

Running an amusement park was very different from operating a tramway system, yet it was only in December 1910 that the tramway company decided to leave the entertainment business. It was then that a consortium of local showmen set up the West Riding Amusement Syndicate to buy and run the park. The asking price was £21,000 but the new group was unable to reach that figure and a compromise was reached when the syndicate took out a lease as from February 1911 and appointed as manager a Sheffield showman, William Mottershead, on a salary of £250 a year with free accommodation in the Lofthouse Park Lodge.[9]

Mottershead stayed for nearly three years, but keeping the interest of the public was becoming too difficult for him and he resigned in October 1913. Earlier in 1913 there had been an article in the *Light Railway and Tramway Journal* which gave warning that the novelty of tramway-company operated amusement parks as in America soon waned and the same could happen at parks like Wakefield's and Edinburgh's Portobello. The article suggested that such parks were better run by men of the show and entertainment world than by tramway companies. It would seem that the 'West Riding' was also beginning to find this unfamilar side of its business difficult and had decided to get out of it. Shortly after Mottershead's resignation the park's assets and liabilities were sold to three gentlemen for £5,000. The park closed at the end of 1913, for the expected success of a small zoo had not been realised and the public were no longer interested in the amusements there.

However the park was soon to take on a new lease of life. The beginning of the Great War provided the government with the

Figure 8. The pavilion at Lofthouse Park after the fire in 1922. *Courtesy of Raymond Colley.*

problem of where to place the many German nationals who had made their homes, and had businesses, in Britain. Lofthouse Park seemed ideal for a camp where these internees could be kept away from places of national security and, later, protected from the anger of loyal citizens.

The sinking of the liner *Lusitania* in May 1915 seems to have made the authorities act more rigorously in regard to German-born residents in England and by that date the numbers in the camp had swelled to 1,322 with 122 Austrians and three Turks. Many of these internees had been wealthy businessmen. Some of them were from Wakefield.[10] There were at least 40 from the Leeds area. The internment camp was regarded by the authorities as a privileged one for a 'superior class' of people, with many of the internees being able to pay for better food and accommodation. The camp was under the general supervision of the commander of the Northern District with Lieutenant-Colonel F S Low in command of the camp and Major E T Lloyd as his deputy. The internees organised the camp, with numerous committees which were responsible for food, entertainment and management at prisoner level. 'Lowery' and 'Markel' committees, dealing with funds set up early in the war to provide assistance to needy prisoners, were quickly established and the benefits were distributed appropriately. There was an Austro-Hungarian committee to look after people from those two countries. Other committees related to sports, thearicals, the Y M C A, the kitchen, and the camp more generally, The kitchen committee looked after the running of the messes and the camp committee dealt with the internal management and affairs of the camp.

An infirmary was established under a doctor, four R A M C orderlies and sixteen German attendants. The kitchens had a staff of 34 cooks. The camp was split into three sections, South, West and North, as feeding nearly 1,500 people from one kitchen would have been impossible. South Camp had three head cooks and eight assistants; North Camp had three cooks and eight assistants and West Camp had two cooks and ten assistants. Food was supplied in accordance with the government ration of the day but the more affluent were able to purchase additional meat, fish, fruit and vegetables from local suppliers. Many of the poorer internees made small gardens in front of the huts to provide themselves and their families with fresh vegetables at little cost.

The activities in the camp were also organised by the internees themselves, and again affluent members were able to purchase tools and materials for woodcarving, painting and drawing. Lectures were organised on a wide variety of subjects, including language study.[12]

Although the people were held behind wire, it seems that the authorities did not see the internees as a threat to the safety of the realm. Route marches were organised for the men three or four times a week and they would often, on passing Lofthouse School, toss sweets, coins, and even tennis balls for the children to scramble for. The sweets had to be inspected by a teacher before being consumed in case they had been 'doctored'.

An exercise yard was being used as well as a three-acre field that would be available in mid summer. The eight tennis courts were in demand, weather permitting, and if they could not be used there was a well equipped gymnasium.

It would seem that the relationship between guards, locals and internees was on a tolerant footing, as some of the prisoners at that time might have had only a slight connection with Germany, but it needed very little to break the tolerance which the native English had for the German, although locals might well have done business with some of the internees before the war. One instance of feeling generated against the Germans occurred when prisoners were being exercised outside the camp near Lofthouse and were mown down by a driver from Patrick Green Munitions Factory who had only that morning heard of the death of his brother.[13] Yet in the peculiar circumstances of war, one English-born soldier found himself guarding his German-born interned father. Was there a 'no fraternising' rule applied to them as well?

R P Rhodes, when a young soldier home on leave, was asked by his father, the village policeman, if he could help out one evening in a nearby shop filling in food records. In the quiet of the evening he became conscious of a faint thumping that seemed to be coming from out of the ground. He naturally reported the fact to his father, who dismissed the noise as cows or horses in the field at the other side of the road pawing or stamping, for surely nobody could tunnel under the barbed wire and roadway. On returning to camp at Hartlepool he was on guard duty when a telephone flash came to them informing all forces of a break-out by three men of Lofthouse Park by tunnelling under the road.[14] One can imagine how the soldier teased his father when on leave again.

Robert Clark, a Quaker from British Columbia, visited Lofthouse Park P O W camp as a representative of the Friends' Emergency Committee, set up by a Meeting for Suffering, a Quaker organisation, to see to the needs of the internees, especially wives and children.[15] He found much to do as many people had little means of occupying their time. This committee provided books and magazines, woodworking tools, timber, leather-working and book-binding equipment etc, so that those who were not financially self-supporting had the means to help themselves with their newly-learnt skills.[16]

On 8 and 10 October 1918, the civilian prisoners were transferred to Camp IV Knockaloe, again a 'privilege camp', and those who agreed to pay eleven shillings per head weekly could enjoy better food, service, linen and china.[17] There were internees at Lofthouse Park when the war came to a close in November 1918, and when the last of the Germans were repatriated from Knockaloe in September 1919 that may have been the end also of prisoners and prison camp at Lofthouse Park.

Some Germans died whilst at Lofthouse and were buried in Lofthouse Cemetery. In 1960 their remains were interred by the War Graves Commission in the German War Graves Cemetery at Cannock Chase, Staffordshire.[18]

With no entertainment taking place at Lofthouse Park, Lofthouse Park Ltd. ceased business on 13 October 1916 until after the war. Little or no maintenance was carried out during this time so when the park was handed back to the company the grounds and buildings were very neglected.

The Park was taken over by five Lancashire businessmen in 1921 who hoped to rebuild, refurbish and reopen it to the paying public but on 22 April 1922 the wooden pavilion caught fire (at the time it was believed that this was caused by men who had trespassed to gamble) and the fire spread to other buildings. The Wakefield City Fire Brigade was notified but, as the Park was outside its area, its officers refused to attend and as there was no other available and adequate alternative, the structures were left to burn, lighting up a large area of the surrounding district and the large crowds who had gathered to watch. On inspection the buildings were found to be too badly damaged to make the Park a viable proposition again and it was left to fall into decay and oblivion with only a few lupins to remind of the days when it was the Queen of Entertainment. (Figure 8) In the 1930s Roper Brickworks moved into the Park and across the road. The area again became semi-derelict until it was made into a depot for a West Yorkshire Engineering Division.

Bibliography

Issues of the *Wakefield Express,* 1908-1922.
Pickles, W, *The Tramways of Dewsbury and Wakefield,* 1980.
Tramway World and Railway World, 2 July 1906.
Banks, W S, *Walks about Wakefield,* 1871
Rhodes, R P, *Going Back a Bit,* Book 2
Bailey, L, *Craftsmen and Quakers*
Report from the officials of the American Embassy to Sir Edward Grey, 16 June 1916
Roberts, G, *Natural History of Lofthouse and Neighbourhood 1882.*
Beavis, J and Newsome, P, *Time Was...in Lofthouse*

Notes and References

1. Registered on 4 April 1905. There had been eight other companies with ideas for a tramway in Wakefield between 1900 and 1904. Of those only a) Pritchard, Green and Co, Birmingham 1899 and b) Drake and Gorham Electric Power and Traction (Pioneer) Syndicate Ltd, 1900, came forward with definite plans but these failed to materialise.
2. Dick, Kerr and Co Ltd.
3. The Wakefield and District Light Railway Order 1901
4. He married Catherine Hanson, daughter of Captain Ralph Hanson of the 66th Regiment. Benjamin was left the estate in 1838 and died in 1846. His son Charles inherited Lofthouse Park.
5. Pole no 133. Notice to motormen and conductors issued on 15 April 1909.
6. This house had previously been occupied by Mr Metcalf, Chief Constable of the West Riding prior to Mr Andrews.
7. *Wakefield Express,* 21 June 1912.
8. Robert Blackburn had built two all-metal monoplanes by 1911.
9. There were Hagenbachs, Hoffmans and Zieglers in the Wakefield area at this time and they would have come into this catchment.
10.. The Public Record Office, Kew. Ho/45/10947/261042
11 Generally 150 internees with four or five soldiers would walk through Lofthouse, Carlton, Ouzlewell Green, Lee Moor and on to Canal Lane and back to camp.
12. Sunnyfield housing estate.
13. Leslie Baker wrote *Craftsman and Quaker* about his father, James T Baily, the Industrial Superintendent at Knockaloe Internment Camp, Isle of Man, 1915-1919.
14. Small items such as blotting pads and writing cases were made and sold in the area.
15. There were towards the end of the war some 25,000 internees and prisoners.
16. For several years flowers were placed at these graves by local people with money sent from Germany.

14. POP, CRISPS, BOATS AND CORN:
REDISCOVERING WOOLLEY DAM AND MILL

by Brian Elliott

DURING THE EARLY 1940s, before he was married, my father was a regular visitor to Woolley Dam, cycling there with friends at weekends and on fine summer evenings (Figures 1&2). He would swim across the water, carrying a few pennies tied in a handkerchief, used as payment to hire a boat, avoiding a walk from the changing area. Although, as we have already seen in Pearl Putscher's article, the dam was unfortunately drained by the then new National Coal Board in the autumn of 1951, but there are still many fond reminiscences concerning swimming, boating, fishing, picnicking and of course courting, because the area was such a popular and convenient location – at a time when a trip to the seaside was a special

Figure 1. Fred Elliott, Agnes Stone (left, soon to be his wife) and an unknown woman at Woolley Dam, 1940s. The wheel of a cycle is just visible.

Figure 2. A group enjoying each other's company at Woolley Dam in the 1940s. My mother, then Agnes Stone on the left.

Two girls, Winifred Newman and Kathleen Barber, enjoy a day at Woolley Dam. *Courtesy of Freda Newman*

event. Some people will remember the tearooms, the ice cream man and his donkey, the fruit seller, crossing the dam on the chain ferry, discovering freshwater clams, riding on the swings and roundabouts, and the garage that repaired visitors' motorbikes.

In Kath Parkin's 'Memories' feature of the *Barnsley Chronicle*, Harry Owen of Gawber recalled the enterprising exploits of brothers Arthur and Ernest Sergeant who had apparently taken a lease on the dam from the Woolley estate in the late 1920s.[1] The launch of their first boat, which they had made using mahogany planks and copper nails, sank 'like a stone'. Not to be outdone they returned to Wakefield, sensibly taking advice from a professional boatbuilder and afterwards assembled much

Figure 3. The Sergeants' house at Woolley Dam, later known as *The Willows*. Mrs Sylvia Sergeant is pictured left. *Harry Owen*

Figure 4. Mill Lane, outbuildings of Mill Farm and the Seckar valley, c.1974. *The Author*

Figure 5. Site of the old corn mill. The Willows can be seen on what was the damside, in the upper part of the picture. The showman's caravan is an unusual feature, c.1974. *The Author*

Figure 6. Part of the mill outbuildings, now renovated as *Woolley Mill Cottage*, c.1974 . *The Author*

Figure 7. The extent and curved form of Woolley Dam can be seen in this recent (June 1998) view, taken from the former turnpike road (A621 Wakefield Road), the woodland area in the foreground marking the edge and site of the old dam bed. Mill Farm can also be glimpsed on the right-hand side of the photograph. *The Author*

more 'seaworthy' craft. The brothers sold huge quantities of pop during the summer, along with crisps, chocolate, sweets and cigarettes, from the converted house that they had strategically sited – partly on stilts – by the dam wall, together with diving boards and associated facilities (Figure 3). According to Harry, it cost nine old pennies to take out a boat for half an hour; or a shilling for an hour.

Figure 8. This old picture postcard (c1920s ?) gives a very good impression of the remarkable scene by the 'Tea Room and Playground' (Mill Farm). A queue of at least thirty people waits for boats; also of note are the converted railway 'huts' on the fieldside and the donkey and icecream seller, just visible in front of the right-hand railway box. *Coutesy of Chris Sharpe/Old Barnsley*

MILL FARM

The charge for a swim was three pennies a day. The dam had become one of the most popular recreational sites in the Wakefield-Barnsley area.

More than twenty years later, when the present writer taught at Royston Comprehensive School, he used to organise sponsored walks that took students through Applehaigh, Notton village, down Mill Lane (where honeycomb weathering was very evident on the walls of the outbuildings of Mill Farm), past the old mill site and the building that once served dam visitors, and onwards across pleasant countryside to Newmillerdam, returning to Royston via Chevet (Figures 4-6). One of his students who lived at 'Woolley Dam' – in a property known appropriately as *The Willows* – was subsequently able to arrange for him a visit which included sight of the dam wall and a collection of artifacts, mainly cod bottles, retrieved from the legendary 'bottomless' lake.

Rediscovering the area in the summer of 1998, whilst preparing this article, was a fascinating experience. Walking along Wakefield Road carrying a large-scale OS map and aerial photograph, the periphery and the extent of the former dam could still be identified, despite the growth of woodland. Mill Farm can also be glimpsed through the trees, on the hillside (Figures 7-9), though it

Figure 9. Mill Farm: the west front photographed by the author in c1974. The nineteenth century extension on the right (south) side once served as the Tea Room for dam visitors and a table by the lower view was much sought after, offering customers a superb view of the water. This view can be usefully compared with the picture postcard (Figure 8).

Facing the farm from the Wakefield Road entrance. Beyond the reeds can be seen the team rooms and people sat on the grasss bank as shown in Figure 8. *Courtesy of Freda Newman*

The Dam was ideal for boating, and was a popular pastime for those visiting the area. *Courtesy of Freda Newman*

Figures 10a & b. Mill Farm, east front, towards the end of renovation and restoration work.
Courtesy of Martin Lowe

is hard to appreciate that at an earlier period part of this interesting building once served as the Tea Rooms for visitors, only a few yards from the water's edge, where queues waiting to hire a rowing boat formed and where visitors paraded on a grassy 'playground'. The present owners have, since 1988, carried out a remarkable and very sympathetic renovation and restoration of the house, outbuildings and also some of the damside fields, creating a haven for wildlife in the process (Figure 10 a & b).

The southern tip of the crescent-shaped dam passed under the old turnpike road and entered the former pleasure grounds of the Wentworths at Woolley Park. Here, just over the wall of the former

Figure 11. The re-flooded area of the old dam: a tremendous achievement of the owners. *The Author*

estate boundary water is still extant, near to where one of two park waterfalls once entertained aristocratic visitors. Nearby was the park icehouse which was stocked from blocks of ice cut from the frozen dam. Further north, almost at the junction of Wakefield Road and Woolley Mill Lane, more water amidst overgrown willows is still visible. The most surprising change, however, has occurred around the old mill/dam site which now comprises several private dwellings. At *Dam House* the new (post 1994) owners, clearly having an interest in the history and conservation of the site, have also achieved a most remarkable landscape transformation, executed with the advice of all relevant authorities, dredging part of the old dam bed and recreating a good stretch of water (Figure 11). Once again, the area thrives with wildlife and visual interest.

'Woolley Dam' actually straddles the modern parishes of Woolley and Notton but the water corn mill itself lay within the old township of Notton which, together with Woolley (with its chapel of ease) and Chevet formed the northern part of the extensive and ancient parish of Royston. The aerial photograph (Figure 12) referred to above, taken in July 1966, provides us with a very clear picture of the crescent-shaped dam site which, as we have seen, remains a distinctive landscape feature. We can also see the close proximity - via Mill Lane – of Notton village to the south-east. Smaller topographical features such as Seckar Dyke are less easily identified but the mill site and Mill Farm are more evident, especially when the aerial view is compared with the first 1:10,560 (six inches to one mile) Ordnance Survey map (Figure 13).

The most striking feature of the local landscape in and around Notton is the presence of several springs, small streams and wells. Such features undoubtedly influenced early settlement since adequate water supplies were essential for both animals, crops and of course man. Not surprisingly, a practical use of watercourses was in the form of water-powered mills such as Woolley mill which were common even before the Norman Conquest. The mill at Worsbrough, for example, was mentioned in the Domesday Book and, very exceptionally, has survived to be a working museum.[2] Interestingly, another water corn mill – under the same manorial ownership as Woolley Mill – was once extant just to the south of Notton village – at Applehaigh or 'Abbaldy', where a minor stream, Applehaigh Syke, was adapted and a small farming and quarrying hamlet developed, probably from an Anglo-Saxon foundation. Here, the stream would have provided power for at least a few weeks of the year. Thus, locally, and indeed elsewhere in this mainly lowland area it would be no exaggeration to state that few valleys escaped adaptation by water-power during the post-medieval centuries.[3]

The purpose of the two Notton mills was to provide a place where villagers and tenant farmers were obliged to take their corn for processing (at a cost or toll in kind) for use in domestic baking and livestock feed. Traditionally millers were regarded as somewhat shady characters since cheating on measures and tolls occasionally came to light - and of course such deeds were unfairly extrapolated to all, hence the saying that 'hair grows in the palm of an honest miller'.[4]

Although natural advantages were obviously essential in the siting of water mills, accessibility was also vital. Applehaigh was within half a mile of the village and although Woolley mill was about a mile from Notton it was also within relatively easy reach of Woolley village, therefore served contiguous manors.

Where the Dam once was

Figure 12. Aerial view (21 July 1966) of Woolley Dam (crescent-shaped woodland feature), Notton village to the South-East, Woolley Park to the South-West.

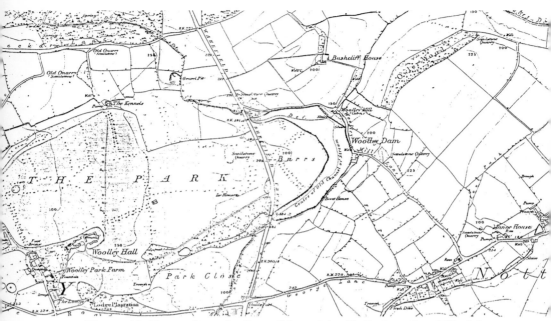

Figure 13. Extract from the first edition of the Six Inch to One Mile OS Map of 1852.

Returning to view our large-scale OS map, we can see that the water course that powered the Woolley corn mill emanated from a spring at about 275 feet in Seckar Wood, flowing in a south-westerly direction and creating a marked valley profile about half a mile downstream at the corn mill site (Figure 14) where there is a confluence with a minor stream which moves northwards where it joined Bleakley Dyke, the township boundary with Chevet. Seckar Dyke itself continued south-westwards from the corn mill, passing under the Wakefield road and into Woolley Park where it was harnessed for water features and a pond. It is highly likely that a corn mill had been located in the Seckar valley, perhaps reliant on the natural availability of the stream and a small millpool or strip of water from at least the later medieval period. A search through sixteenth century probate records at the Borthwick Institute of Historical Research at York has revealed an interesting reference to Woolley mill. In his will made on 4 February 1575/6, Richard Sotheryne of Notton, bequeathed to his son, John, the 'interest and term of years I have at Wolley Watter mylne' subject to an annual payment made to the testator's widow, Agnes, of 'six mette [a measure, also known as a 'strike', usually of two bushels] of Wheate and Rye...at Christmas...and Easter...', such 'payments' ending if Agnes remarried.[5]

The most prosperous local residents in the medieval period were the Woodroves who had settled in Woolley in 1377, buying the house of the prominent lawyer Sir William de Notton but from 1490, having purchased the manor of Woolley, were resident in the old manor house. It was this family that created the fine hunting park which was subsequently incorporated by the Wentworths in the pleasure grounds of Woolley Hall.[6] The Woodroves' large estate also included the manor of Notton and it was probably the last manorial lord, Francis Woodrove, who leased the Woolley mill to Sotheryne.

The writer has found some references about the mill during the seventeenth and first half of the eighteenth century, some more tentative than others. The substantial probate inventory of Sir George Wentworth of Woolley, for example, taken in 1660, includes a small number of items, valued at £5, under the heading 'Goods at ye Mill delived to George Hutchinson', namely

two kilne-hayres, 4 chests, one gavelock (iron crowbar)*, 24 picks, 2 milne chessell, one Axe, one dusting sieve, one Range with a payre of Pullese & ropes, a fann & other remaynes* [7]

Figure 14. Bushcliff House/Farm can be seen on the hillside overlooking the minor stream that flows northwards to join the Bleakley Dyke. The valley profile here, near the confluence with the Seckar Dyke and Corn Mill site is quite steep. *The Author*

The presence of so many picks and a 'gavelock' may seem somewhat incongruous but, as we shall see, these were almost certainly employed in one or more of his lordship's coal pits. A little later, in 1675, Woolley resident Richard Webb described himself as 'milnwright' suggesting that there was sufficient local work for this ancient craft.[8] Webb appears in the hearth tax assessments of 1672 and a John Hutchinson appears in the Notton returns. The vast collection of post-medieval papers of the Wentworths of Woolley, housed at the Brotherton Library, University of Leeds, provides us with further sources of information about Woolley mill. The family had come to Woolley in 1599, purchasing the hall, park and manors of Woolley and Notton from Francis Woodrove. In a deed dated 19 January 1706/7 William Wentworth, esquire granted to John Foster, husbandman, a coal mine 'on Woolley Moore near Bimshaw' along with 'two Corne Mills Woolley Mill and Appleday Mill in the township of Notton' at an annual rent of £62, plus 80 wain loads of coal and 25 capons, Foster – a notable local coalmaster – agreeing to leave the mills 'in good sustinance [and] tenable repair'.[9] At the same time a 'Schedule' or inventory of both mills was drawn up, the Woolley mill list then consisting of:

> *one new kilne haire*
> *one lock and key on kilne door*
> *one ridle for ashes*
> *one Dragg and new stroake* [dry measure]
> *two Corn Arks* [large wooden storage chest] *in ye Mill & Lock & Key*
> *one malt tubb with lock an key*
> *one dozen of picks*
> *one Gavelocke* [crowbar or lever] *iron*
> *one milne Chesell & great Hamer*
> *one Hatchet & one spade*
> *one halfe Peck & quarter*
> *one cable rope bell rope & Pullies*
> *one old bedstead*
> *one water fann* [for winnowing grain] *& one habd fann*
> *one dusting sive & dusting board*
> *one locke & key to ye Milne door*
> *one moulter dish*
> *one new siche and fire Rainge* [10]

Most items clearly relate to milling but again we see the presence of a 'gavelock', picks, ropes etc, suggesting that Foster was storing some

Figure 15. James Brindley, 1716-1772, the pioneering civil engineer, who was responsible for more than 360 miles of canal in England. His famous aqueduct over the river Irwell can be seen in the lower left background of the portrait.

of his mining tools and equipment there; also interesting are the two references to 'locks & keys', a reminder of the importance of security at such 'public' sites. A smaller number of items were listed for 'Appleday milne'.

Much later, in 1749, Godfrey Wentworth commissioned Arthur Scott to produce a 'Plan and Survey' of Woolley in which we find that the mill's tenant was then James Redfearn, though interestingly no dwelling house is recorded at the corn mill site.[11] This James Redfearn 'of Woolley Mill' appears in the Royston burial register of 1762, so he was probably the last tenant of the old mill prior before its transformation by one of the most creative and prolific civil engineers of the day, Mr James Brindley (Figure 15).

Brindley's commission – to design a new mill and dam – has been dated to 1765, but this may have been the completion date.[12] Certainly, Brindley was consulted as early as 1755 when he wrote to

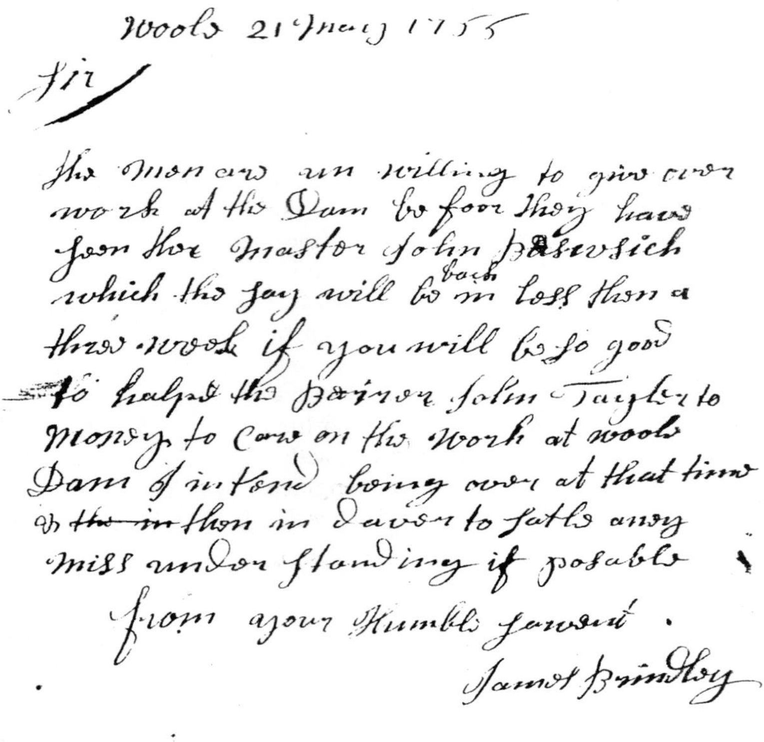
Wools 21 May 1755
Sir
the men are un willing to give over
work at the Dam be fore they have
seen thar master John pakesich
which the say will be back in less then a
three week if you will be so good
to help the Bainer John Taylor to
money to carr on the work at wools
Dam I intend being over at that time
& ~~the in~~ then in daver to sattle any
miss under standing if posable
from your humble servant
James Brindley

Figure 16. Letter from James Brindley to Godfrey Wentworth, dated 21 May 1755 *Brotherton Library, University of Leeds, Wentworth-Woolley Hall Papers, 1949/1*

Godfrey Wentworth, describing certain labour problems (Figure16).[13] Wentworth's choice of Brindley is a most interesting one. He would have undoubtedly have heard of his successful record via the aristocratic network of the day and more particularly because of Brindley's triumphant and creative project (1760-61) for the Duke of Bridgewater, when a canal linking the Duke's coal mines from Worsley to Manchester included the Irwell aqueduct, regarded as a 'wonder of the age'. Brindley had also been consulted locally with respect to the Calder and Hebble navigation (1764) and, earlier (1760) by the river Don company.[14] As a young man he had worked as a millwright, so the Woolley project may have had personal appeal. Brindley's engineering projects were notable for creatively transforming local landscapes and this was certainly reflected in the graceful shape and proportion of the new dam at Woolley which must have been regarded as a spectacular feature compared with the modest stretch of water that it replaced; and yet there is some evidence to show that his patron was far from happy in the aftermath of the engineer's work.

In fact relations between Brindley and Wentworth became somewhat acrimonious, the engineer apparently threatening a lawsuit. Wentworth responded in no uncertain manner, writing to Brindley on 14 December 1768, from his favoured house at Hickleton: 'I am surprised you should say, you have nothing further to do with stopping the water, when you must be sensible, that this was the Principle object of our last Agreement', ending his curt reply with 'I shall forbear to take any notice of the incivility of part of your letter as I don't find my self in the least hurt by it'.[15]

In school textbooks and encyclopaedias Brindley is generally regarded as an intuitive, practical engineer, the following quote, taken from the the *Cambridge Encyclopaedia* of 1990 being typical:

> *An illiterate, most of his* [Brindley's] *problems were solved without writings or drawings.*

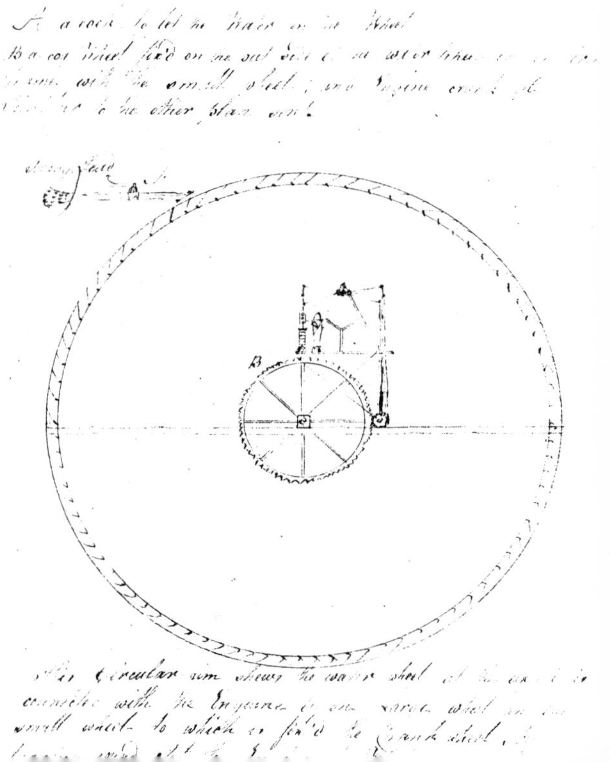

Brindley's letter to Wentworth, though crudely written could hardly be described as 'illiterate' and his interesting technical drawing of Woolley mill (Figure 17) suggests a more than basic grasp of draughtsmanship. A fine pen and ink map by Brindley with the legend *A Plan of the Proposed Canal, for opening a Communication between the Ports of Liverpool & Hull,* is also extant amongst the Wentworth-Woolley Hall papers.[16]

Whatever the outcome of the differences between Wentworth and Brindley, the new corn mill and dam appear to have been oper-

Figure 17. Brindley's drawing of the water wheel and its associated mechanism. *Brotherton Library, Wentworth-Woolley Hall Papers.*

ational for at least a further hundred years. An Elizabeth Peaker, for example, 'daughter of the Cornmiller of Notton' is recorded in the Royston parish register for 1813. Turning to the census enumerators' returns for 1841 we find that Richard Peaker ('aged 60'), living with his wife, Francis, a 'Male Servant' named Andrew Learoyd and a child ('aged 5') called Emma Stead, is listed as 'Corn Miller' at 'Woolley Mill House'.[17] This 'Mill House' was not located at the mill site but a short distance away, at what later became known as Mill Farm. The 1706 'Schedule' of mill items mentioned above only

Figure 18. Extract from the 1843 Tithe Award Map for Notton. Three 'Windmill Close' enclosures can be seen to the west of Mill lane. *Borthwick Institute of Historical Reseach, University of York*

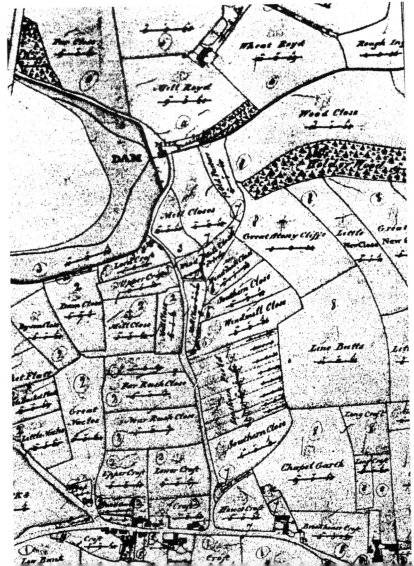

includes reference to a single 'fire range' and bedstead, so accommodation at the mill may have been either primitive or non-existent. The present Mill Farm, on architectural grounds alone, has features possibly dating back to the seventeenth century, and certainly eighteenth century. This building, set on the hillside, but with more space compared with in the Seckar valley, was clearly used as a residence for the miller, with outbuildings used for storage, and would also have enabled him to keep a few farm animals and grow some crops. The only other dwelling in the vicinity was Bushcliffe House, farmed in 1841 by David Pickard.

However, the presence of the miller's house on a hillside, away from the mill may have been for long-fogotten but historic reasons. If we consult the 1843 Tithe Award map for Notton (Figure 18),[18] just to the south of Mill Farm, on the east side of the lane, three small hillside enclosures are named as 'Windmill Close'. The sites of windmills can often be identified from the air by a circular mound and ditch. The mound supported the the 'legs' of the mill whilst the ditch marked the spoil pit from which earth was extracted. Such earthworks, however, may have been levelled but still revealed by crop marks, which show construction trenches, usually in the form of a cross enclosed by a circle.[19] On an extract of our aerial photograph of Notton (Figure 19) a feint circular feature of this form is just discernible – in one of the former 'Windmill Closes' – and would be perhaps more visible from an oblique angle. Three or four footpaths leading to the feature are also evident. This could certainly be the site of a long lost and unrecorded ancient mill, pre-dating the water-powered mill lower down the valley.

This article, albeit a short study, provides the local historian with

Figure 19. Enlarged extract of the Woolley Dam aerial photograph of 1966. The tip of the arrow touches the edge of a circular crop mark (with a cross in the centre), probably indicating the site of a medieval windmill. Four paths appear to radiate from the feature.

an opportunity to combine family and oral history alongside local history; to combine the use of field-work, maps and also aerial photography with documentary research; but there remains much to discover – both ancient and modern – about this small and fascinating corner of the old West Riding.

Acknowledgements

I am very grateful to Mr & Mrs H Piper and Mr and Mrs M Lowe for allowing me to visit their properties; and for all their help and kindness. Thanks and grateful acknowledgement is also due to the archive staff at the Brotherton Library (University of Leeds) and Borthwick Institute of Historical Research (University of York). My thanks also to Kath Parkin at the *Barnsley Chronicle* , Chris Sharpe of *Old Barnsley* and to my father, Fred Elliott. Thanks also to Paul Wilkinson and Freda Newman for additional photographic sources.

Notes and References

1. *Barnsley Chronicle*, 30.5.97
2. For information about Worsbrough Mill see R Shorland-Ball's article *Worsbrough Mill Museum*, South Yorkshire County Council (reprinted from *Industrial Archaeology Review*, vol 11, No 3, Summer 1978); also *Worsbrough Mill Museum*, Martin Watts, South Yorkshire County Council (nd); and for a brief account see B Elliott, *Discovering South Yorkshire*, Smith Settle (forthcoming).
3. For an excellent group project see David Crossley (ed), *Water Power on the Sheffield Rivers* (1989); and for the Dearne catchment area the work of Tom Umpleby, see, for example, 'Water Power Sites in the Dearne catchment' in Elliott, B (ed) *Aspects of Barnsley 3*, Barnsley, (1995).
4. Taken from G Grigson's *Geoffrey Grigson's Countryside*, Ebury Press, London, 1982, p 244; for an excellent oral history account see chapter 14 'The Miller and the Millwright' of George Ewart Evans's classic study, *The Farm and the Village*, Faber and Faber, 1969, pp 142-153.
5. Borthwick Institute of Historical Research (University of York), St Anthony's Hall, York, Registered Wills, Vol 22 folio 73.
6. Geoffrey Markham's *Woolley Trail* remains an excellent topographical guide to the village and its principal families: Bretton Hall and Wakefield Metropolitan District Council Architects and Planning Department, revised edition, August 1975, pp 4-5.
7. Brotherton Library (University of Leeds): Inventory of Sir George Wentworth, Wentworth-Woolley Hall Papers (hereafter WWHP), MS Dep 1946/1/16.
8. Borthwick Institute of Historical Research, Registered Wills, vol 56 folio 153.
9. Brotherton Library (hereafter BL), WWHP MS Dep 1949/1 33/10.
10. *ibid*
11. BL, WWHP, MS Dep 1949/1 / 25.
12. Markham, op cit, p 1.
13. BL, WWHP, MS Dep 1949/1/ 104.
14. Hadfield, Charles, *The Canals of Yorkshire and North East England*, vol 1, Newton Abbot, 1972, p 51 7 p 77.
15. BL, WWHP, MS Dep 1949/1/104.
16. *ibid*
17. Public Record Office, HO/107/1324.
18. Borthwick Institute of Historical Research, Notton Tithe Award (1843).
19. M W Beresford and J K S St Joseph, *Medieval England An Aerial Survey*, 2nd edition, Cambridge, 1979, pp 64-65.

CONTRIBUTORS

1. THE STORY OF RHUBARB
9. A 200-YEAR LEGACY OF THE 1793 WAKEFIELD INCLOSURE

John Goodchild is a native of Wakefield and was educated at the Grammar School there. He has been active in local historical research since about the age of thirteen, and is the author of over 140 books and published essays on aspects of the history of the West Riding. He was founder-curator of Cusworth Hall Museum and subsequently Archivist to Wakefield MDC; in his retirement he runs a Local History Study Centre which houses his immense collection of manuscripts and research materials, and which is open to use, free of charge, by appointment. Mr Goodchild holds an honorary M Univ from the Open University, awarded for academic and scholarly distinction and for public services. He is a regular contributor to the *Aspects Series*. Outside historical research, his interests lie in Freemasonry and in Unitarianism - and his dog.

2. IMAGES OF WAKEFIELD

Antonino Vella was born in Wakefield in 1960 of Italian and Sicilian parentage. He was educated locally at St.Austin's R C Junior and Infants School, St Thomas a Becket's Comprehensive, and Cardinal Hinsley R C Grammar School, Bradford. In 1981 he gained a first-class honours degree in the History of Design and the Visual Arts at the University of North Staffordshire, Stoke-on-Trent. He also has a post-graduate diploma in Museums Studies. Nino has been Keeper of Art at Wakefield Art Gallery since 1986.

3. MY DRINK IS WATER BRIGHT

David Scriven moved to Yorkshire, where he now teaches history at Batley Grammar School, after studying at the University College of Wales, Aberystwyth. He has been interested in local history for more than twenty years and is a founder member of the Ossett Local History Society. He has carried out research on the social and economic development of Ossett in the nineteenth century and has given numerous talks on the subject as well as having an article published in *Old West Riding*.

4. BRAMWELL PASHLEY AND PEGGY TUB MAIN

Keith Wainwright is the son of a mining surveyor and lifelong inhabitant of Crigglestone. He was educated at his village church school, Wakefield Academy, Highfields Grammar School and Whitwood Mining and Technical College. Employment for the whole of his working life has been in local government, initially in the County Mining Engineer's department of the former West Riding County Council, and subsequently with South Yorkshire County Council and the Barnsley, Doncaster and Rotherham authorities' joint Mining Department, SYMAS. For the past twenty years he has been responsible for the compilation of an archive of mining information covering the whole of the county of South Yorkshire. This archive, comprising a register of over 22,000 mining and mining-related plans, is second only to the Coal Authority's archive at Bretby, Staffordshire. He is the author of numerous historical studies of Crigglestone and district and is presently researching the history and involvement of Crigglestone 'Tommies' in the Great War. Married with two grown sons, his other interests include fell walking, rugby, photography and his local church, St James, Chapelthorpe, where he is Sacristan and where he has sung as a chorister for the past fifty years. He is currently chairman of the Crigglestone Parish Council.

5. Wakefield's Garden City Schemes
11. Shirts from Wakefield

Coral 'Kate' Taylor was born in Wakefield in 1933 and educated at the Girls' High School before going on to St Anne's College, Oxford, where she read English Language and Literature. After teaching in Leeds, at West Park C S School and the City of Leeds and Carnegie College of Education, she took up a post as Principal Lecturer in

English at Wentworth Castle College of Education at Stainborough. Following the closure of the College she became Vice-Principal (Community) at Barnsley Sixth Form College when it opened in 1979. Since her retirement in 1990 she has spent her time researching local history, in particular in the field of entertainment. Her book *Right Royal: Wakefield Theatre 1776-1994* was published in 1995. She works part-time as a tutor for the Open University and is the Hon Managing Editor of Wakefield Historical Publications, President of Wakefield Historical Society and Chair of the Mercia Cinema Society. Kate has written articles on theatre history for *Aspects of Barnsley 4* (1996) and *Aspects of Doncaster 1* (1997) and is currently editing the forthcoming first volume of *Aspects of Wakefield*.

6. The Poplar Avenue ACC Club

Marjorie Pearl Putscher (nee Olson) was born at Stannary Hall, Halifax, a seventeenth century house owned by Crossley's Carpets, where her father was chief engineer. She attended Holy Trinity Infants School and Crossley and Porter's Grammar School. She attended Heckmondwike Grammar School and Thornes House Grammar School. In 1944 she joined the WRNS straight from school. In September 1946 she obtained a Social Science Diploma at Leeds University. In 1948 she became a child-care officer working in Lincoln and later in the Dewsbury area. Her hobby is the theatre and she is a founder member of Wakefield Little Theatre, a trustee of Wakefield Theatre Royal and Opera House, a tutor for the U3A (play reading) and a member of the Matcham Club of Great Britain.

7. A FIELD IN BELLE VUE AND 13. LOFTHOUSE PARK

Peter I Wood was educated at Normanton Grammar School from 1944 to 1949 and served in the RAF before returning to work for a local engineering company. Later he went to Scawsby College of Education and then taught in Pontefract. He has been a member of Wakefield Historical Society and its council for over twenty years and became a vice-president three years ago. He has written and published a school history and the Sandal History Trail. He is currently involved in the preparation of a book covering Belle Vue, a district of Wakefield. He is involved with the U3A and walking groups and is very interested in local history. He has taken part in study days for schools and archaeology open days at Sandal Castle and has undertaken enactments there. He is married with a son, and is a grandfather.

8. BASTARDY IN OSSETT

Ann Barnes was born in Leeds, at 'Jimmy's', in 1944 but spent most of her childhood in Selby. She was educated at a boarding school in the village of Hillam, at Selby Girls' High School and at Wakefield School of Commerce. Her BSc degree, from the Open University, was obtained whilst she was not only working full time but also raising four sons. Her paper on Bastardy in Ossett was first prepared as a project for the Open University course *Studying Family and Community History* (DA301). For more than a dozen years she has worked in the Local Studies department at Wakefield library headquarters. Her interests, apart from local history, include crosswords, competition, cookery, crochet and crafts.

10. THE PRACTICAL VALUE OF RESEARCH

Ronald Swinden JP was born in Wakefield in 1923 and educated at St.Paul's Elementary School, Alverthorpe, and Thornes House Boys Secondary School. After serving as a clerk with Wakefield's Blind Welfare Department, he was employed in various clerical positions by the LMS Railway Company before joining the RAF in 1941 where he served as a wireless operator with the Air Sea Rescue Service in India, Burma and Hong Kong and went on in 1946 to become Educational and Vocational Training Instructor at Saharanpur, India. Postwar employment at the West Riding Registry of Deeds led to his engagement by the Wakefield solicitors, Dixon, Coles and Gill. A lifelong Methodist, he was the Sunday School Superintendent at Westgate End Methodist Church and later at Wrenthorpe Methodist Church where he pioneered the building of a new Sunday School, 1973-8. He served for 33 years as a magistrate until reaching the age bar of 70. He is the president of Wakefield Burma Star Association and treasurer of the Voice of Methodism association. He has written and published *The Burgoyne Saga* and *The Origin and History of Kirkhamgate*.

12. THE CREAM OF HOSPICES: THE FOUNDING OF WAKEFIELD HOSPICE

Alan Kirkbright was born in Yeadon and educated at Aireborough Grammar School and Bradford University where he studied Pharmacy. After qualifying as a pharmacist he served in the army in an Ophthalmic Unit of the RAMC. Following his discharge from the forces he studied Medicine at Leeds University and after qualifying entered general practice in Wakefield where he has lived since 1954. He combined general practice with an interest in Ophthalmology and has been an ophthalmic medical practitioner for more than thirty years. He and his wife are active supporters of the Hospice movement. His book, *It's a Doc's Life*, is a collection of anecdotes based on recollections extending from childhood to his retirement from general practice in the 1960s.

14. Rediscovering Woolley Dam and Mill

 **Brian Elliott** was born in Royston and spent his childhood in the village of Carlton where he attended the primary School, and then Edward Sheerian School at Athersley. After an undistinguished spell as an apprentice professional footballer he obtained a proper job, working for Barnsley Corporation in a Dickensian office next to the Public Cleansing Department. Whilst Head of Geography at Royston Comprehensive School he also tutored adult education courses for the WEA and University of Sheffield and published short histories of Royston parish. He researched his own town for an M Phil, awarded by the University of Sheffield in 1990. His popular book *The Making of Barnsley* (1988) was the first published historical account of the town since 1858. Brian founded the acclaimed Aspects of Local History series, edits *Aspects of Barnsley and Aspects of Doncaster* and advises Wharncliffe on local books. Recent publications include *Barnsley's History From the Air, 1926-1939* (1994), *Barnsley's Sporting Heroes* (as editor, 1997) and *Discovering South Yorkshire's History* (forthcoming). Articles on Barnsley's photographic history have recently been published by the Royal Photographic Society. Brian works at Rother Valley College where he is Head of School (General and Community Education).

INDEX OF PEOPLE

191

INDEX OF PLACES